Another Day, Another Miracle

Ceil McLeod

Tyndale House Publishers, Inc.
Wheaton, Illinois

Coverdale House Publishers, Ltd.
London, England

Cover photo: James B. Gross
Library of Congress Catalog Card Number 74-21964
ISBN 8423-0072-4, cloth
Copyright © 1975 by Tyndale House Publishers, Inc.,
Wheaton, Illinois 60187. All rights reserved.
First printing, July 1975
Printed in the United States of America

CONTENTS

Introduction

If we are to believe commercials, a woman with a suburban home, two cars, bright children, and a comfortable social position has succeeded. Happiness should be her domain. But success, as the world views it, is no promise of joy in living.

The dearth of joy can be attributed to a large extent to the impersonal nature of our lives. Look what has happened in one generation. The walk to church has become a drive to a citadel anchored in asphalt. The community store with its prune and pickle bins ripe for tasting, is now a giant shopping center. The turreted home with its hideaways has become a sterile cubicle, too small and noisy for grandparents.

Instead of playing baseball on vacant lots, kids heavy-foot car accelerators or enroll in organized activity instead of creative play. No longer is the wisdom of the aged passed down. Too often the nursing home is distant and is incompatible with the bounce of youth. Add to this generation gap the computerization of lives in a jungle of electronics so vast that man feels helpless to untangle himself, let alone the computers' errors, and you have desperately lonely people.

I was one of those lonely persons and, for me, meaning came only after a long struggle in which I sought to find peace with God. I found I needed the whole fabric of God in a crisis world both for myself and my family.

My story of seeking this wholeness in God would be more dramatic if I had been an alcoholic, a prostitute, or a heroin addict. But perhaps because I am an ordinary woman without such dramatic sins, my search will more closely mirror that of others. All Eve took was an "apple" in a garden, yet she evoked a life sentence of eviction. God cared about a stolen "apple." He cares about us each time we turn from him momentarily.

Once yielded to God's Spirit, each of us can be rubbed into shining newness and then drawn into exciting adventures beyond our dreams. For all of us, the miracle of God's touch on our lives is fresh with each new day.

ONE God's Looking Glass

Once in the life of every woman comes a moment of truth alone with a mirror. Looking in my mirror, I thanked time for the becoming white streaks flaring at my temples and for the plumper me in contrast to my adolescent days when no curve softened my yardstick figure. But God's mirror has a way of showing the inadequacy of a person—that is, if we dare to look beyond the reflected glass image. For a moment I was face-to-face, looking in God's mirror. I knew God saw under the wing-tipped hair into the tangle of my life.

When had my glowing girlhood dreams of becoming a missionary dimmed, I wondered. It began when I entered into the social gaiety of my husband's sales world. Without realizing it, to avoid being called a prude, I had enveloped my real self with plastic layers. It is only when a moment of truth shows us ourselves reflected in God's eyes that we feel choked in a web of our own wrapping.

My moment of truth blossomed one warm spring evening not unlike many others in suburbia. Dusk crept in as my husband, Hugh, and I strolled down curving Heather Lane. We looked back to wave to our children on the porch of our home: Gail, with the awareness of nineteen and searching eyes of an artist, and Hugh III, with the angularity of eleven and the warmth of one who loved people. They were handsome children, I

11

thought, full of promise. I loved them—their weaknesses and their strengths—a part of me. Why shouldn't we be proud? Hugh had worked hard for our graceful home standing well back from its fashionable curb. We really have it made, I thought.

Hugh took my arm. "You're pretty as a peacock tonight, honey," he praised. I strutted like one. Only a woman would care that the gown I wore was as exquisitely finished inside as outside, but he liked it. That is what mattered.

Downhill meant uphill in Avondale's social ladder. The landscaping had a natural look instead of being merely a clump of planting. The lower houses and swimming pools became increasingly luxurious.

When we reached our hosts' colonial home with its pillared veranda, gay laughter rushed at us as the door opened. Our eyes blinded at brilliance from chandelier prisms reflected on diamond earrings and smiling faces. For a second I wondered why wealthy people are so often beautiful.

Our hostess called, "Oh, there you are, you two. Come in. Come in. We're all starving."

As she urged us toward the dining room, our near neighbors, Connie and Ted, asked what we thought about the PTA Follies in which Connie had participated. We knew Ted wanted us to comment on Connie's slender loveliness among the mostly dimpled knees of the cancan line. We did.

"What's this I hear about you being president-elect of Eastwood Parents' Club next year, Ceil?" Connie asked.

"Oh, that. Hardly anyone knows me over there. They don't know whether I'm left or right, and that seems to be an asset these days. The job sort of scares me, though. I don't know much about education, that's for sure."

Soon all eight guests and our host and hostess were seated around a table fit for King Farouk, from buttercup-patterned Limoge china to delicate crystal that chimed to the touch. When the last chair had been pushed in, our host raised his brimming double martini glass. "Bottoms up," he challenged, grinning.

"Bottoms up" with double martinis! I looked for Hugh's reaction. He seemed as surprised as I. This was a fast crowd, but the pace had quickened, it seemed. Glasses were emptied, except mine. I raised mine, but sipped little. In the first place, I didn't like the sour-bitter taste of martinis; still, they were too potent to down like water, even if a person did like them.

In the midst of a discussion about the symphony, our host noticed my dawdling. "We're all ready for another, Ceil. Empty your glass."

I mumbled something like, "Have to watch out with martinis." I was glad he ignored me when another tray of double martinis was passed around. I waited impatiently for the food to be served. Would it never come?. . . Not before the group had another round of drinks. Decibels of sound later, mouth-watering Chicken Divan and trembling molded raspberry salad appeared. The food was delicious, but only Hugh and I seemed to notice. The rest were too high to be hungry. As I ate, I wondered why such affluent, successful people needed to drown themselves in martinis. Drunkenness this night was to be no accident, but a planned occasion. Even my fun-loving husband failed to appreciate the deliberate bacchanal proceedings.

I looked around the table. These were church-attending parents including a young Catholic couple, parents of six children, opposite me. When dinner was finally over, about an hour later, we were invited to the sunken party room where a bar on wheels magnified what had become raucous hilarity.

Music blared a jungle beat. Locked couples swayed. Holding a rancid-tasting drink, I talked into the smoke haze around our host. A violent movement by the fireplace caught our attention. The young father of six had become a volcano of action. His body writhed in a suggestive motion that lurched and swung in front of our hostess. As the tempo increased, so did his body's action, until he seemed an animal acting out an orgy of passion.

Embarrassed, I turned toward his wife, but her back was turned. I wondered how she could bear it. But then, how could her husband behave like this in front of everyone? Suddenly I felt angry. I remembered his library of great books that shaped his keen legal thinking, books by Aristotle, Plato, and Tolstoy. Something within me rebelled at having to pretend I was having a "ball" when I wasn't. But with long practice at the social cover-up, I smoothed my face and began to plan how soon we could leave.

Before I could catch Hugh's eye, a flash of color at the top of the stairs startled me. Were those children in pajamas peering over the railing? "Go away," I wanted to shout. They mustn't watch that awful dance.

Suddenly all the wealth, prestige, and power in that room closed in on me. Was this all we were living for? Was this the heritage we wanted to pass on to our children?

Nothing moved now on the stair landing, but what had the children seen? I felt dirty and guilty, for wasn't I part of the view from the stairs? Catching Hugh's eyes on me, I nodded toward the door. For once he was as ready to leave as I. There was no need to make farewells. No one noticed us slip away.

Once outside, Hugh grasped my arm. "What's the matter, honey? You look as if you'd seen a ghost. Are you sick?"

Swallowing over the lump in my throat, I mumbled, "I've never been so sick—inside, I mean. I never thought I'd be a part of a party too ugly for children's eyes."

"There weren't any children there."

"I'd swear I saw some little figures peeking over the stair landing. What if it had been our children who saw that drunken dance?" Tears stung my eyes. "If only I could wash it all away in a shower," I spoke through clenched teeth.

I tried, but the shower only cleansed the outside. Inside I felt as if layers of scum sloshed and jogged and seemed to shout, Is this what you really want, Top-of-the-Mark living that leaves you bereft inside?

After Hugh finally fell asleep, I checked our children, but the ache didn't subside. I began to think . . . When and where had we left God? How had we reached this point? It had been so gradual that I hadn't even realized our personal climb had really been downhill, away from God, away from all the teaching of my childhood.

Easing into bed, I watched the moon's pattern, laying a silver streak over the hump of my husband's knees. Dear Hugh, I thought, he loves parties and an exciting life, but in many ways he's more stable than I am for all my puritan attitudes. I should have listened to him that night months ago when we, with Connie, a church deaconess who had also attended the party, gave way to curiosity and attended one of Billy Graham's Crusades.

My face flushed with the memory of Connie's words, "You know, if either of you had made a move, I believe I'd have gone forward. I had the strongest urge to do so."

"What do you know," Hugh smiled at her. "I did, too. Billy Graham seems for real in spite of his thunder."

Walking beside them down the stone steps, I mused, Why hadn't I felt the same urge? Wasn't it because I felt I was closer to God than they? At this sickening pious reaction, I blushed; my lips moved, "Dear God, what a phony I am, righteous on the outside and sick of myself on the inside. Half the time I'm real and half the time I'm somebody else." Months later I found the Apostle Paul felt much the same when he said in prison, "For the good that I would I do not: but the evil which I would not, that I do" (Rom. 7:19).

In the hushed bedroom I seemed to hear the words Billy Graham had spoken that night at the Crusade as plainly as though he stood on our turquoise bedroom rug. I could even feel his piercing eyes on mine as he said, "All too many church people wear masks of self-righteousness."

As I lay in bed beside Hugh, Billy Graham's words faded, but not their message. He's right, I thought. Just to be a good sport or to be part of the crowd, we don't have to pretend to smile at dirty jokes, drink to be a "good Joe," or be a good neighbor by going to parties like the one tonight. God wouldn't want me there. I'm sick of being a social pretender. It was then I made a decision: From now on I'll try not to see anything I don't want my children to see. Somewhere in the dusty corners of my mind the words returned, "For what shall it profit a man, if he shall gain the whole world, and lose his own soul?" (Mark 8:36).

The room was still and God seemed near. I began to pray. "I don't know how to get back on the track, God," I began, "but at least I know I don't have to pretend to like what you dislike. No longer must I worship on the altar of popularity." The longer I prayed, the more I felt relief engulf me. Finally I relaxed and slept.

The next morning as I dusted our living room, my thoughts wandered back to summer days spent in my Grandmother Riggs's laughter-filled New England home with its three flights of curving stairways. God had been a part of all we did then. My earliest recollections begin in that Victorian parlor with my brothers, Steve and Bill. There Grandfather Riggs, after breakfast that often included fragrant blueberry muffins, always read from the Bible, knelt, and led us in prayer. Sometimes during the long prayer we peeked at his strange upturned shoes with their stubby toes. We knew his shoes had to be specially built around his toeless feet, and that his toes had been frozen long ago when he was a missionary to the Sioux Indians. Squinting my eyes, I could almost picture him back in Minnesota, staring down at his frozen, gangrenous toes, miles from the nearest doctor. He must have prayed hard before plunging his hunting knife across those oozing toes. Someone had to bandage the bleeding stumps. I wondered if he had to do this, too. He looked sort of small and bent in the New England parlor, but he must have been mighty brave back then in the wilderness.

But it was really Grandmother from whom I learned most about God. She had the real glow. Grandmother was warmly alive. Love issued from her like steam rising from a warm street after a thunderstorm. Though dust never had a chance to gather in her stately home, she always took time for stories, games, and music. Even though she dressed plainly in starched dimity and huge aprons, to us she was the most beautiful grandmother in the world. She smelled of raspberry jam and lavender. Smiles crinkled around her mouth and eyes. We knew from her that she depended on God for all her needs and that he provided. I knew the glow was wrapped up in dependence on God and the Bible, but I wished now that I had asked her all the questions that bubbled up in me before she went to be with God.

Perhaps if I went back over the years, I could discover where I had begun to take the wrong turns and somehow reverse the process. A seeker needs a plan, a path, or at least a lantern. Grandmother was a road sign.

My oily dustcloth lay forgotten while I gazed out our tiny-paned window toward flowering redbud trees in the distance. Just as the trees had faded while I recalled feeling prickly spikes of horsehair from Grandmother's sofa, now New England misted away while I found myself seated on a hard pew in an Illinois hand-hewn chapel. I strained to listen, for here was another who knew of God's intimate secrets. A lovely Japanese girl stood before us, glowing like an iridescent butterfly. How simply she confessed, "I am three years old today." What a silly thing to say, I thought. She's at least twenty-one years old. She continued, "On this very day three years ago in Tokyo a missionary spoke to me and some of my high school friends in her home. She told us about Jesus and how he said, 'Except a man be born again, he cannot see the kingdom of God' (John 3:3). That day my life changed. That was my birthday in Christ."

I wanted to ask, What does it mean to be born in Christ? But even as I thought about her, the "other me" began to rationalize. After all, she was formerly a Buddhist. Naturally, the Christian story would be strange and wonderful to her and completely different from anything she had ever known. It's her oriental background that makes it all seem so wonderful.

Come now, I argued. You know differently. That girl had something you want desperately, but don't know how to find. Oddly enough it was like the children's story by Maeterlinck, *The Blue Bird*. [1] Now I, too, was searching for something just as hidden and impossible to find as the blue bird. I thought I knew all the entrances to the Christian life—baptism, joining the church at twelve, teaching Sunday school, and leading women's work—but none had led into God's inner room. What were those words? "Seek ye first the kingdom of God, and his righteousness; and all these things shall be added unto you" (Matt. 6: 33).

I had become a seeker, but where would I find the answers? Many people I knew seemed to be imitators of Christ; they knew the ropes and played the pew-sitting game, but they, like me, could turn God off as nonchalantly as they do an alarm clock and go about their business. I knew suddenly that it wasn't enough to take food to the sick, or to raise funds for underwear for a girl's orphanage. All this is great. It is clean living, you're helping someone, and you mingle with nice people; but it is only Christian life by imitation. Fine, but I asked myself, How do you get the real thing? If I could sort out what made Grandmother and the Japanese girl different from others, perhaps then I could find the key.

There was a time when I felt the glow—at a campfire at Lake Sunapee, when I was fifteen. I remembered watching flames reflect in a twisting dance on the quiet water at the church camp. The moon spun a wavering path into a clump of pines on the shoreline. Once again I seemed to breathe the pine-scented air as I listened to the words of the visiting minister.

"In the heart of some girl here tonight is a dream, a dream of serving God. Christ said, 'I am the light and the truth and the way. Rise up and follow me.' You may be the one to be a lantern to others if you follow Christ's call. Tonight you may become one of Christ's committed. The answer is in your heart."

As he sat down, the favorite words of *"Onward Christian Soldiers"* marched across the water in soft girls' voices into the moonlit path and hurled themselves into the fragrant breeze.

Sitting cross-legged, I hugged my long legs tightly to me as I searched my heart. A soldier for Christ. Yes, that's what I'd like to be. . . . Where do you sign up for such an army?

When I returned home, Mother was glad to hear of my camp adventure, but when I told her of my proposed induction into Christ's little band, she smiled and said, "That's wonderful dear, but you will be a better soldier after you finish high school."

A thump of mail dropping on the tiled hall floor startled me. Heavens, it must be noon, and I haven't even cleaned one room. God's looking glass had revealed yesterday's faces. When would I learn today's answers?

TWO **A Small Valise**

But this Christian soldier went AWOL. I fell in love with Hugh McLeod, a young man from a different world. Mother's words as she studied his picture on my desk both influenced and puzzled me. "I like his face, dear."

"But there is something you wouldn't like," I blurted, expecting her to look shocked. "He smokes and drinks."

"You'll find there are other things more important than that. There is something fine and good in his eyes."

Two years later, during my sophomore year at Simmons College, my mother died suddenly of a blood clot following surgery. From then on I spent vacations with my father in New Jersey, a father I scarcely knew from the time of my parents' divorce when I was twelve. Long ago their worlds had clashed: his, the social life of the son of a vice-president of a Boston bank; my mother's, the staid world of a missionary daughter.

Hugh's background was more like my father's, but he had a wonderful kind of gentleness. All his life he tried to please those around him—his grandmother, his widowed mother, his sister, his boss. I knew I could count on his kindness. Somehow I never questioned whether he tried to please God. He belonged to a respected church. That ought to mean something.

Though but five feet nine inches tall, his stride was that of a six-footer. I like that, a go-getter, a doer, a climber. I wanted to climb with him. It was many years before I realized ours was no Jacob's ladder to the heavens. We were climbing our own, and some of the rungs were wearing thin.

Two years after my mother's death I became Mrs. Hugh McLeod. No husband could have been more loving when serious illness hit—first our baby daughter, Gail, then a floating kidney for me. Hugh secured the only surgeon in the country then who could suspend a kidney to the muscles of the back. With this surgery I was restored to active life, and active it became. We danced to the business "fiddle"—parties, drinks, and sometimes drunks. The latter I never could stomach. Hugh took it as a fact of life. Inevitably conflict began.

Those days I dressed to attract. One evening at a cocktail party at our home I wore iridescent taffeta that rustled and shimmered, changing from emerald to sapphire in candlelight. Petal sleeves clung to my arms framing bare shoulders. It was a dress to set men aflame and I hoped it would. Not dangerously, that would never do, I told myself piously. It did attract. A young father, new in our set, hovered like a moth, sending glances I enjoyed receiving. Fearing it would become obvious, I rushed to the kitchen for hors d'oeuvres, proud of my self-control, little concerned with his.

The day following the party, his flaming red convertible drove alongside my baby's carriage as I pushed it down the twisting Pennsylvania lane. No gossip could have found crisp tidbits. We talked quietly of family things. But I knew what his eyes said. He knew I liked the message.

Nothing came of it, but lust was there, lust encouraged. Oddly enough I came through such times preening over my nobility in keeping everything in control. Only later did I see myself as God saw me, breaking down my pretenses finally even from myself.

No man can serve God and mammon too, the Bible says (Matt. 6:24). It doesn't mean you can't try. Both of us would have been stunned if anyone had suggested our ways were unchristian. While God seemed close when I was gathering raspberries in the fields, he seemed far away at sales gatherings.

We waited eight years for Bruce to happen; five months of it I spent in bed. He was a beautiful baby, but needed immediate corrective abdominal surgery. In nine days Bruce returned to God as gently as scarlet leaves fell from our catalpa tree. God gave and he also took away. It was hard to understand, but he sent an answer. Some young people from our Methodist church begged us to start a Sunday evening group (later called the "Round Tablers for Christ"). It seemed that they had been turned down by all the likely church leaders. We agreed to serve. They never knew how their loving response and enthusiasm helped to heal the hurt of our baby's loss. While they thought we were helping them, we found fulfillment.

But how could Sunday's youth leader be reconciled with Saturday's peacock? Increasingly, I felt torn by the two directions my days took. I longed for peace, but it seemed just out of reach. Meanwhile, God sent our son Hugh, who had his dad's love for people and always seemed God's own child.

Years have a way of passing. As our daughter finished her junior year at high school in Indiana, we began visiting colleges. At this time I read an article in a national magazine that really shook me. The magazine did a survey of ten outstanding colleges, including Jewish, Catholic, Protestant, and a state university, to determine those in which young people's religion maintained itself, grew, or diminished. The greatest loss of faith occurred at the Protestant-oriented school. It hit me for the first time that my children's faith must be unshakable, or it might be lost in their college years. Here was a situation I found I couldn't handle.

How many times had young Hugh said, "Let's read the Bible together, Mom." And I had taken this lightly. It was as though a searchlight shone glaringly on my whole relationship with God. It wasn't a sham, for I had tried over and over to be like Christ, but it was pitifully shallow. How could I really know him when I scarcely knew his word? How could my children stand tall in him when they saw me turn to God only in emergency panic times? Our mumbled table blessings could hardly penetrate their young lives with strength against the lies and deceit of those who would destroy their very faith.

I realized for the first time that the only lasting gift I could give my children beyond my love was a demonstration of my own deep faith in God. In this I knew I had failed, yet I couldn't understand why. I'd used all the ordinary channels. Ah, but God is not ordinary. To just believe isn't to have power to sustain others.

I was struck at the core of my being. I saw danger to my children and was powerless to help them. I must find and gain this power, and time was running out. Gail would soon start college.

Young Hugh and his friend, Jimmy Berling, were already trying in their boyish junior high way to reconcile the scientific theories of their brilliant science teacher with the Sunday school teachings of their church. I couldn't even help except to say, "I believe."

At this time my activities as president-elect of Eastwood Junior High School Parents' Club put me on a committee under the Washington Township Board of Education to investigate secret social clubs in the community. We soon found that some of the socially prestigious clubs required, for membership, acts like thefts (confirmed by stolen goods) and sexual promiscuity. As we dug deeper, we were warned by the high school principal that we might be slandered. But we persisted. Fortunately we had a former FBI member working with us who handled legal encounters. When our investigation results were finally printed and distributed throughout the school district, the press praised our courage in publishing the truth, parents thanked us for warning them of the facts, and a Presbyterian minister preached a sermon on the hazards youth encountered.

I had experienced forces desiring to cover up evil. But this was only a part of the problem. About this time, our son, who had never missed Sunday school, refused to join the junior high group. Puzzled, I began to read his lesson book. One lesson especially disturbed me. It seemed to me make a child question his faith in God, not grow closer to God. I took it to our minister. He read the lesson, frowning thoughtfully. At the end, he turned to me. "I agree with you, Mrs. McLeod," he said. "Unless the teacher is highly skilled, such questions to junior high young people could damage their faith."

Incredibly, at the same time, I read a paper our son wrote on Lincoln that seemed derogatory rather than a eulogy. I couldn't believe it. Rounding up library books on Lincoln, we took off for Lincoln's boyhood home in southern Indiana. On the drive down we read aloud tales of the great emancipator. We walked the paths he had walked.

For three days we stepped back into history, touched by the future greatness of the boy, Lincoln, much the same age as our own son. On our return I studied Hugh's textbook.

As early as page five I found gossipy statements and later a description of sexual activities that should have no place in a schoolbook about a national hero. Such remarks lent no new truth or even relevance. Rather, it seemed a sort of sticky flypaper innuendo to cover the strength of Lincoln's innate honesty.

Again I rushed with my notes to our junior high school principal. A man of integrity, he expressed shock at these needless inclusions in a schoolbook. He, in turn, passed the information on to the school librarian who was equally disturbed. I was informed that as textbooks are revised from time to time, items may be tucked in or deleted. Since the task of rereading all books is a giant one, some things may be overlooked. However, parents may help review books through proper channels, and changes may be made through study.

I was grateful for the cooperation of both school personnel and our minister in studying teaching materials, but became increasingly aware of a sort of undercover campaign to poison our children's minds. Unlike the classic Western, the true villain was unclear and unknown.

In addition to these experiences, I found groups determined to get Weekday Religious Education out of school planning. How many other forces were marshaled to attack my son's faith both in God and our country's heroes? I didn't know. Most of my friends seemed content to play bridge as usual. For me, time had run out. The alert was on.

My comfortable world was splitting wide open. I felt responsible and helpless at the same time. But in the next few days I was to become even more helpless.

Another Day, Another Miracle

A few weeks after the culmination of those disquieting events, as I bent to turn off the vacuum cleaner one day, I felt a sort of elastic snapping in my lower back, so like the twisting feel of life when I had carried our babies. Pain, extreme pain, followed until one week later when I awakened, I was unable to turn or sit up. Believing I could break the grip if I stood on my feet, I hauled myself up in an agony of pain only to dissolve into unconsciousness. In brief moments of awareness I saw the worried faces of my husband and son, Hugh, floating above me.

I was soon hospitalized. The doctor's diagnosis: a herniated disc. On my return home, I wore an ugly corset with two one-inch steel wedges up the back. Though improvement followed, eight months later the silly thing snapped again while I was shoveling just one small step of snow. Another doctor ordered a body cast from armpit to below the hip bone.

In the cast, I now resembled a sawed-off caterpillar, an awful plight for one whose dresses were designed for an hourglass figure. I finally settled for maternity dresses. For seven months I appeared on PTA platforms in expectant mother clothes. When I finally went back to the hospital for a spinal fusion, my friends could hardly wait to hear if I had given birth to a boy or a girl. What a letdown to learn I had only given birth to bone fragments in the seventh lumbar area.

We'd tried all the cures for a herniated disc—brace, plaster cast, heat. Now an intricate surgery of removing a knob of spinal bone, crushing it, and inserting it in place of the completely destroyed disc promised new life for me.

In my spiritual life, I, like the doctors, had tried all the usual processes of becoming a Christian only to find no cohesive force, no spine of God to hold my spiritual life together.

I didn't leave the hospital in the expected ten days. Instead, I began having terrible muscle spasms as the nurses helped me walk. I was unable to sit up without support and then only in a reclining position. As the pain grew more intense and specialists consulted together about my condition, so my loneliness for God also intensified. But my pride kept me from telling anyone how I felt.

Our minister visited. Waving a list, he mumbled, "Let's see,

A Small Valise

I have three in Community Hospital, two at Methodist, and one more on this floor."

Appraising his harassed face, I reassured him, "I'm fine." Putting a pleased check mark by my name, he hurried off. A Christian friend brought me an armful of books, all black and religious looking. These she tucked embarrassedly into a bureau drawer while she talked about something else.

I soon became used to the tinkling bell of the priest of Saint Joseph's Hospital. He appeared in the early morning to administer Communion. As he served my roommate, he noticed the question in my eyes. For a few mornings he drew an imaginary cross on my forehead. But again, the gesture failed to satisfy my inner craving.

No one spoke of God. No one questioned how I felt inside. And I couldn't ask, for to ask was to say, "Look here, I have worshiped God all my life, but I find he's a stranger, and I don't know how to open a door and get to know him. I'm lonely for him, desperately lonely, and there is really no one to ask. You give me the trappings. I've had all that. How does one go about learning to know God?"

My nightstand overflowed with candy boxes, flowers, and a racy book—efforts on the part of friends to cheer me up.

Weeks slipped into months, bringing no reassuring medical progress. Hugh's cheerful smile became forced, his shoulders slumped. Young Hugh's boyish phone calls halted. Who could blame him? He had given up calling after the time a muscle spasm made me scream into the phone halfway through a sentence. Few letters came from our daughter, Gail, at Purdue University. She was having her own battle, between studies and a quarrel with her boyfriend. Knowing her to be the kind who spilled over with good news, but kept bad news to herself, I couldn't help worrying about her. As the pain grew, so did my detachment. I felt unable to buoy up the spirits of my family as was my wont. I knew for the first time what it meant to wander in the wilderness. Only my wilderness was a white bed. I had given up looking for someone who would search my eyes and say, "My dear, what is troubling you?"

Then one Sunday, November's fading sunshine lay in a warm

spot on my bed. Two and a half months of Sundays had passed slowly. There was no promise that this would be different. Even the tinkling of the priest's bell, proclaiming early mass, passed by our door this week, for my new roommate, like me, was of Protestant persuasion. No one but God knew of the hymns that flashed through my thoughts, wanting to be sung, but the idea was soon abandoned. A solitary burst of hymn singing might cause a patient to be moved quietly out of the orthopedic section into one more appropriate, I thought. Turning in slow motion in order to prevent the torturing muscle spasms, I faced the empty door and another empty day.

Soft steps approached in the corridor, soon turning toward our door. Two middle-aged men in business suits greeted my roommate. I noticed one carried a small black valise of an odd shape, neither a suitcase nor a briefcase. After speaking quietly to my roommate, the taller man who was nearly bald and had smile crinkles around his eyes, opened the case on our dresser. He laid out a small silver tray and placed on it four tiny glasses. As he caught my puzzled look, he introduced himself, and said, "We're laymen and have come today to share Communion with Mrs. Arnold. We wondered if you would like to join us."

So that's what it was! I glanced up at his friendly face. "Oh, I'd love to join you." I had no idea whether I was supposed to take Communion given by some unknown church and administered by laymen, but I was sure, even if my church board objected, that Christ, knowing my spiritual starvation, would approve. Maybe he had sent these men to comfort me.

The man who had talked to me read concerning the breaking of the bread and drinking of the cup. Christ's words, "This do in remembrance of me" (1 Cor. 11:24), hit me for the first time. For a moment sunlight flooded the shabby room. I realized the four of us, until now strangers, were a church. Didn't Christ say, "Where two or three are gathered together in my name, there am I in the midst of them" (Matt. 18:20)?

Christ was our host. As I thought about him and the gift of his life on the cross, I felt his presence fill the room.

After the men had gathered their things together and gone, I realized I had said little except, "Thank you." I was sorry, for now they would never know what sharing their simple commemorative act meant to me.

In the month ahead, I struggled through painful corridors of agony, until a day when the muscle spasms began slowly to ebb in severity. As my body sought release from pain, my heart sought a loosening of its bonds of spiritual silence.

Months of searching and prayer brought Christ's presence nearer. I knew finally that God was with me in my search to be closer to him. He had sent the two men to me in my loneliness. Who would he send in the days ahead? Who would lead the way to a better understanding of God?

THREE Yoked into Glory

Meanwhile, other changes were ahead for us. In my long months of recovery at home, I had much time to think and read. We were thrust into the civic spotlight as our son won the *My Pop Is Tops* contest with his boyish letter describing a dad never too busy to listen to him, one who participated in Scouting with him. This brought TV and a Mayor's presentation honoring my husband as Indianapolis "Father-of-the Year." As this faded, our daughter married, her love having endured five years of college. Friends who knew of the limitations of my back helped entertain out-of-town relatives during wedding festivities.

Social events aside, I turned for answers to my church circle. I knew from their worn Bibles and excitement in Christian things that several of our group had the inner track with Christ. Sometimes I felt guilty because my questions disrupted the planned circle program, but I felt I had to find out what they had.

Unfortunately, before I could add up any answers, my husband was called to Cleveland. He returned with the unwelcome news that we were to move to Saint Paul. Within one week he was transferred there, leaving me with the selling of our home. To me, selling a home is a bit like selling the children. I had already sold five homes, usually just as the trees were beginning to give shade and the rose garden was bursting into a blooming oasis. But this time was even harder. I was on a God hunt. Wouldn't it be more difficult in a strange place?

On prior moves I had urged Hugh, "Be sure to find a lovely home, just right for antiques and in the best school district." But this time I begged, "Never mind school or house. First, find a church where God is evident."

"And just how do you do that?" he asked hopelessly.

"I really don't know, but I think it has something to do with conservatism. And let's see . . . they ought to believe in the Trinity and the Virgin Birth. Be sure to ask a lot of questions about Sunday school materials, too."

Poor Hugh, he knew what to ask about schools and houses or church buildings and choirs. But this doctrine thing . . . what a task. Months passed with the home still unsold and Hugh no closer to the church thing, though he had heard some great sermons and glorious music in Saint Paul.

In desperation six months later, we sold the house at a whopping loss, determined at least to end our family separation. Five days prior to the moving van loading, with no destination in sight, I remembered a little gray house on a hill, too close to the highway behind it. Its chief lure was a sign on a vacant field one block away that said "Future Home of Saint Paul Bible College." The next day, in the midst of packing books, I smoothed Hugh's sleeve. "Honey," I pleaded, "why don't we buy that little gray house near the Bible college? There ought to be some Christians near there, and it would be so wonderful to know where to unload all our furniture."

"What about the highway?" Hugh asked.

"It's not a busy one and maybe the builder would put in a planting to screen it off. Besides, it's the only house we saw that goes with antiques."

"All right, we'll call the builder. One good thing—young Hugh wouldn't have to change schools twice."

Within an hour, we had bought the house by telephone with the promise of a planting come spring and even with the additional concession that we would move in a day prior to bank settlement. What a relief.

Yoked into Glory

Our "little gray home in the west," as we called it, was cozy and had a charm of its own. Neighbors were friendly and the Arden Hills school excellent. We even discovered we were supposed to be living in the Bible belt. But we still hadn't found a church home.

Days lengthened into February in our comfortable hilltop home. One sunny morning I watched a vagrant cloud bathe a seminary tower in the distance in blue shadows. My problem was like the tower, too distant to see clearly. Following breakfast my Hughs left for school and business respectively.

Leaving dishes stacked for once, I opened Catherine Marshall's book *Beyond Our Selves*.[1] Usually I found some real answers here, but this morning the words were just words. My emotions refused to leap as she spoke of spiritual strength, answered prayer, and Christian fellowship. I knew it could all happen to me, but I needed to be involved with Christianity, not just meet it intellectually. We were weary of church hunting, but where else to go?

We had tried affluence. We had worshiped at a large suburban church with its well-dressed congregation. Nothing was really wrong there—highly-trained choir, dignified sermon followed by friendly invitations to meet afterwards for coffee. A well-preserved man (no doubt a church elder) smiled at me while stirring his coffee. "We're delighted to have you here," he said. "Some say we serve only the wealthy, but that just isn't so." Then in a serious vein his brows raised while his eyes searched mine. "By the way, what did you say your husband does?"

The room seemed too still. I was conscious of the elegant puff of his silk handkerchief. Something in me wanted to shock him. What if I said, "My husband is a janitor"?

The words hung in the air tempting me, but I heard my voice respond, "He's branch-manager of the Addressograph-Multigraph Agency." His brows relaxed. Affability wrapped him in its cloak. "Ah . . . we hope you will make this your church home."

Something in me coiled up. What if we were shabby? Would he have bothered with me? Was there room in the pew there for the hungry and tattered and lonely? We never went back there.

Another Day, Another Miracle

Perhaps we misjudged the church. But one stuffed bosom was enough to keep out many sparrows, we thought.

Then, next, there was the ugly meetinghouse with artificial flowers looped around angled woodwork. Many of the people looked run through a fluff-dry process—in need of ironing. I felt too elegant, too coiffured, too gloved among the working hands and booted feet, as out of place as a Saint Bernard in a cat hospital. The minister had an honesty about him (this might even be real, I thought) but where was the elegant, intellectual climate we were used to? I hated myself for my snobbery, for that is what it was, just as bad as the elder with his silk handkerchief. Maybe we didn't deserve to find a house of worship; that is, if we were too good for ugliness. And so we left that church, aware that truth might be there, but somehow we were misfits.

A tiny little church near a superhighway was friendly. The minister's wife passed an opened hymnal to us with a welcoming smile. The organ and piano leapt into enthusiastic notes, all but rocking the low roof. I settled into my seat. Maybe this was it. The minister, balancing on his oft-shined shoes, announced the return of "Brother B" who had returned from a life of sin to the way of salvation. Up sprang "Brother B," his tie swinging to one side and his hands clutched together.

He gave us a salty description of drunken orgies followed by the flashing moment when Christ took over. Hallelujahs rang out; tears coursed down a few withered cheeks. I told myself, that's great, God. One mark for your side, but we'd have to sow a few more oats to come swinging into this congregation. These were good people, and the change in the man was no doubt remarkable, but it all seemed too emotional. We exited quickly.

How dreadful really to be locked into respectability, to behave like a wind-up toy, always dignified in public. But years in this type of mold made us uncomfortable any other way.

Seven churches visited, and we were still outsiders. If we wanted a neighborhood church for our son, we knew of only one more, Calvary Baptist. I had never been in a Baptist church. My only childhood Baptist friend, Ellie, had often invited me to Baptist socials, but I never went. Poor Ellie. I remembered the times Ellie spent with us, white-faced and quiet after her parents' terrible quarrels. Then the awful suicide of her mother. There I go, I thought, letting one tiny incident influence me. Talk about bias, I had it.

Palm Sunday dawned in bright sunshine with a promise of spring. Still, I buttoned up my brown winter coat in the frosty air. Calvary Baptist Church swarmed with people gathered in friendly circles. A few smiled. We jostled our way through the noisy hall to arrive at the sanctuary door. A beautiful room opened before us. Antiqued pink brick walls gave a feeling of texture and solidity, while golden flecks trembled against the coolness of a turquoise-walled alcove. We learned later that these brass discs suspended above the baptistry were designed to quiver over warm water during baptism.

As I settled into the quiet, I felt an overwhelming peace. This peace I saw reflected in faces around me. My eyes followed huge columns of pressed wood that seemed to grow from the floor up the wall and merge in strength at the ceiling like huge oxen yokes—a mighty support. Seven such yokes held up the vast ceiling.

How long had we journeyed to find a church, to find a way to Christ? This was our last resort, a church and people strange to us, but not strange to the Lord, it would seem.

Though I knew few Bible verses by heart, words from my childhood returned as I sat under the giant yokes. "Come unto me, all ye that labour and are heavy laden, and I will give you rest" (Matt. 11:28). Rest, dear God, a sanctuary from seeking. You know we need that.

The words of Christ came clearly now. "Take my yoke upon you, and learn of me; for I am meek and lowly in heart: and ye shall find rest unto your souls. For my yoke is easy, and my burden is light" (Matt. 11:29, 30).

Tiredness lifted from my shoulders. Something was about to happen. I stared at the three crosses hanging on the wall, one larger than the others, all delicate looking but with the tensile strength of steel.

Choir voices hushed, the young pastor began quietly to tell of the scourging of Jesus: the stripes on his back, that back that carried the burden of the world; the pressing of a crown with thorns that tore into his flesh; his patient loving eyes that looked sadly through dried rivulets of blood. That Christ stood before us and the people cried out, "Crucify him."

We shuddered at the terrible sound as nails pierced bone while his hands and feet were nailed to rough boards; at the pain on his face as his body hung in position. Sun beat relentlessly down on the sagging figure. Then his gentle voice, "I thirst." We saw the Master's dry lips open for a vinegar-drenched rag. His eyes sought the heavens. "It is finished," he said. And darkness fell. The earth trembled in its bowels and people fled. The lonely figure hung there.

For the first time we knew why this terrible death took place. It was for us. Not a story of something that took place two thousand years ago. It was real, and it is real today. He died that we might live. Live how? Live in him.

I was startled to see tears in my husband's eyes, his hands knotted in anguish. He, too, stood at the foot of the cross that moment. We watched Jesus die and it was terrible and beautiful. For it was God's gift to us. What greater gift could he give. I glanced toward my son. His blue eyes shone and he smiled back tenderly. To give up one's son! "Oh, God," I breathed, "thank you for your gift. How can I be worthy of such giving?"

The last hymn note faded. Pastor Frykholm stood below the platform, eyes tightly closed. "Are there any here for whom I may pray? Are there any here who would accept Christ's gift of eternal life, his promise that 'As many as received him, to them gave he power to become the sons of God, even to them that believe on his name'?" (John 1:12).

Both my husband and son raised their hands. I simply could not lift mine, and soon the service ended.

I was the last to come to Christ. My pride broke more slowly than that of my husband and son. I had been so sure that the religious background of my youth made me somehow more pure than others. I can guess now what Jesus would have said to me. "You knew in your Grandmother Riggs a woman deeply filled with my Spirit. I spoke to you often, but you turned away. Does this make you holier than those who never saw me in others?"

When Pastor Frykholm asked the question again two weeks

later, I felt my arm rise, without quite knowing why. Pray for me please, my heart demanded. I want the gift you offer.

Pastor Frykholm came out to talk and pray with us, each separately, for all of us come in our own way to the threshhold of God. When our pastor read with me the words of God, "For all have sinned, and come short of the glory of God" (Rom. 3:23), at that moment I saw myself as God sees me, stripped of my holier-than-thou wrappings. My sins stretched out before my eyes—lustful temptations turned away at the last minute, but cultivated and encouraged all the same; peacock-like clothes designed to allure; selfishness disguised as unselfishness. The muck ran in a flood of pictures. As quickly as it appeared, it vanished, leaving a glory behind, wiped away because of Christ's agony.

Pastor Frykholm's eyes sought mine. He must have seen my revulsion and wondered. Still I wasn't ashamed of the tears that spilled down my face. I was cleansed, purged of myself and my sanctimonious front. What peace!

"God wants you to have life and have it abundantly, Ceil, but there is only one way to the full life. Jesus' way. He put it this way, 'I am the way, the truth, and the life: no man cometh unto the Father, but by me.' (John 14:6).

"Do you want Christ for your Lord and Savior? Do you accept him as the way to eternal life?"

"Yes," I whispered.

"Then let us pray." The love which God has for me echoed in the pastor's tender voice.

My words tumbled out, "Thank you, dear God, for the end of a long search. Now I am your daughter; your Son is my Lord and Savior. I needed you and now we are close."

From that day we seemed lighted like sparklers. The Bible began to talk to us, opening new truths daily. When we bubbled over with questions as we grew in faith, God sent us friends who listened patiently, sometimes a bit puzzled; but friends who told us what Christ meant to them in their lives. I found myself devouring books by Elton Trueblood, Paul Tournier, and C. S. Lewis. How could I have missed these great Christian philosophers so many years?

Another Day, Another Miracle

Months later, as I cleaned kitchen closets, I opened one high cupboard long unused. I was startled at the profusion of long-stemmed glasses and aperitif bottles of deep garnet and lime green. Without even missing it, we had dropped the cocktail hour from our lives. This must be part of the new direction we had been promised. What freedom—never to worry about my husband's late drive home after a sales cocktail party.

On the other hand, we seemed *church programmed:* Sundays from 9:30-12:00, evenings of church, prayer meetings on Wednesday, and evangelistic meetings whenever they popped up. Our car steamed back and forth, and my church dresses began to have pew-seat sag in the back.

For my birthday Hugh bought tickets to *Joan of Arc* at the Guthrie Theatre for all of us. They were expensive, but we had done nothing of the kind for months. From the balcony I watched actors pivot and parade. Usually I could lose myself in the play's emotion. But satire on the church at this time was an attack on my new church. I kept waiting for Joan's revelation of Christ to rock the audience, but, as I should have known, George Bernard Shaw wasn't out to present a revival meeting. We squirmed through the first act.

As the lights went on, our son looked at me. "Do you really dig this stuff? If we hurry, we can still hear part of the evangelist's message at Calvary." With one mind, we scrambled down the steps. As I watched my Scottish husband tearing up expensive ticket stubs, I marveled. Four evenings in a row we had heard the visiting evangelists at our church. Here we were rushing back, afraid of missing one word of Christ's truths. What had happened to the staid sophisticates of a few months back?

FOUR **Manna and Me**

After church one Sunday morning, a young woman invited me
to visit her Bible study group in Arden Hills. She must have
seen me wince at the invitation for she added, "It may sound
dull, but we really have fun together." Her bouncy enthusiasm
persuaded me to attend their next meeting. "We're a mixture of
Presbyterians, Baptists, one Covenanter, an Episcopalian, a
Catholic, plus a few unknowns."

That could be lively, I thought.

It was. In a sunny living room overlooking Lake Johanna, I
felt immediately at home while sipping coffee from dainty cups
with eleven attractive young women. Mrs. Smith, our leader
with wispy white hair and penetrating blue eyes, turned out to
be the wife of a professor at Bethel College. "Isn't this where
we left off—Jeremiah 4:10?" she asked. There was rustling of
pages as a variety of Bibles were flipped open.

Jeremiah, where is that? Old or New? I panicked. I scanned
the index stealthily, sensing a pause as they waited for me. I
turned hastily to page 962 only to discover I had Zephaniah
instead of Jeremiah. Even my neck burned as I fumbled once
more for the table of contents.

Mrs. Smith read smoothly, "Ah Lord God! surely thou hast
greatly deceived this people." There was certainly no deceiving
these people, I thought. All those years of churchgoing, and I

was too dumb to find Jeremiah. When I calmed down, I felt a gentleness among the girls. No one was here to judge me. They were here simply to share love and help each other grow in faith. What a link!

As weeks passed, I came to know the girls well: Annie, the fashion model with expressive black eyes, found excitement in everything; Evelyn, a dynamic leader, area chairman of Christian Women's Club, carried a well-thumbed Bible; Sally, a rebel like me in some ways, had the honesty to say, "Guess I'm stupid, but I just don't understand that passage." How often she spoke what most of us had too much pride to say. I especially loved her for it.

We jumped from Jeremiah to John, and this book I could find. For the verse I claimed for my own was John 1:12 about that thrilling moment when I *received* Christ.

Halfway into chapter three of John where Jesus talks about being born again, Evelyn turned to me. "How long have you been a Christian, Ceil?" she asked.

She couldn't know how I had been agonizing about those very words for I understood Baptists, and maybe all others for all I knew, believed you became a Christian when you publicly repented and received Christ. I wasn't about to admit that I had been an infidel all those long churchgoing years. My pride erupted.

"As far as I know, I've been a Christian all my life," I countered. "However, I've been a newborn Christian only a few months, and of course that's a revolutionary change. That's what Christ is talking about to Nicodemus when he says, 'Except a man be born of water and of the Spirit, he cannot enter into the kingdom of God' "(John 3:5).

"I always thought there was only one kind of Christian, the newborn one," Evelyn added.

I could see the puzzled faces around me and thought they, like Evelyn, were probably right, but I also thought I had a point.

"How about verse 15?" I demanded. " 'Whosoever believeth in him should not perish, but have eternal life.' I can't remember a time when I didn't believe in God and in his Son

Jesus or in eternal life, and I always tried to follow Christ and his teachings. Does this make me a heathen?'' I challenged.

"Certainly not," Mrs. Smith interjected, "but was Christ your Lord and Master then?"

That was the root of it, I realized. "No," I answered. "He wasn't in *control* of my life then; I was. Nor had I seen my sin through his eyes then. I'll admit that I was more an imitator of the Christian way than I was a fulfilled Christian, but I still feel I was a 'kind of a Christian.' "

No one seemed ready to decide on which side of Christ's ledger I had stood until my recent new birth experience, but I was unwilling to drop it there.

"Besides, God sent me special experiences years ago at the time of my mother's death." Now I really had their attention.

"Long ago I had a bridge rendezvous with God." I proceeded to tell about the terrible February night when I returned from a college swimming meet, my wet hair frosted in the cold air. I knew at once something was wrong when my brother Steve, a sophomore at Harvard, opened the door.

"Ceil honey," he began, swallowed, then tried again. "Mother's gone. She died this afternoon."

I stared at him. She couldn't be. I'd rubbed her aching legs at the hospital just the night before and she seemed better.

"It's true. . . . A blood clot passed to her heart. That was what caused her pain." He led me into the hall, tenderly slipped off my coat. "I've been calling relatives." Dear Steve, I thought, he looks as lost as I feel, but he's already shouldering the burden of a fatherless and now motherless family. I must help him, but I've depended on mother so long. . . .

A world without mother was unthinkable, but there it was. Somehow the days passed. Like an actor in a play, I ate, I went to bed, and I attended classes. With Steve's help I managed to dismantle our home. Then Billy, my sixteen-year-old brother, and I moved in as boarders with a friend of mother's while Steve returned to Harvard.

I got through the days mechanically; it was the nights that were nightmares. The thought of being both sister and mother to the boys overwhelmed me. And the aloneness. After our parents' divorce years before, dad had remarried and had become a sort of legend that appeared in brief visits like the one for mother's funeral and as checks in the mail.

Often I lay awake in the black night, fearing to fall asleep as a recurring dream terrorized me. I kept seeing mother with her sweet, patient smile in the background of a misty room or on a crowded street. When I tried to reach her, she vanished then reappeared only to dissolve again. Always after this experience, the loneliness was worse.

On the outside, a pattern of living developed, including Sundays with Steve at our boarding house. Soon Billy learned to darn his socks, while I ironed the boys' shirts, sometimes finding extras from Steve's Harvard roommates in the laundry bag. I tried to answer piles of sympathetic mail, mostly from mother's friends. I was touched by the generous Christian acts they described that she had never shared with us. But somehow the letters only made the ache for her deeper.

Mail continued to arrive, but none from Rick, my boyfriend of last summer. Surely he had received my letters. Five weeks had passed. Then one day an envelope with his schoolboy writing lay on the hall table on my return from college. I read it quickly, especially the line, "Meet me at Boston Garden, opposite the Parker House on Saturday at 12:30."

A quick glance in the mirror indicated droopy hair and deep circles under my eyes. For the first time I realized how gaunt I had become. Sleepless nights, worries over studies, loneliness, and the need to change overnight from dependence to a new independence combined to make me resemble a refugee rather than a Saturday date. Add to this darned stockings and Aunt Can's purple coat dyed green, and I was hardly something out of *Harper's Bazaar*. Well, Rick would understand what I had been through and make allowances, I thought.

But I found out otherwise. I could tell from the way he looked at me that he didn't understand. I could feel each darn and nothing could make the lumpy coat svelte no matter how I wrapped it. We sat restlessly through a stupid movie, then moved out into crowded Tremont street. "Now what shall we do?" he asked.

Watching Rick's fingers sift coins in his pocket, I remembered his slim allowance. "Let's walk in the Commons . . . maybe feed the squirrels."

"Might as well," he shrugged. I'd never been in a city with Rick before. How different it had been last summer at Lake Sunapee. There was a tenderness then in the way he held my hand as we half-ran through a sun-filtered birch grove. How protective he had been, guiding me around lichen-covered rocks. How powerful he had seemed as we swam together far out into the lake. If only he knew how desperately I needed that taken-care-of feeling now.

We soon discovered it was too early for swan boats and even for peanut venders. It seemed winter still held the park frozen and waiting, rather like our summer love. Gray haze settled down. Untidy papers fluttered on the sidewalk under our feet.

Rick glanced at his watch, frowning, "We'd better head back to your place. I have to catch the 4:30 train back to New Hampshire."

So soon, I thought. He seemed in a hurry to leave. But then, maybe I was wrong. Perhaps he had something else on his mind.

Days passed in empty succession without further word from Rick. My brother Steve began to realize I looked wretched. Hoping to cheer me, he arranged a triple date for me with a fraternity brother for the coming Saturday.

Dressed in tiers of high school vintage apple-green ruffles, I watched eagerly for the boys' arrival. Minutes passed, turned into hours. About ready to slip out of my gown angrily, I heard the phone's jangle. What possible excuse could they have? But it was my uncle's voice from Newton Hospital. "Ceil, Steve's here. I'm afraid he's seriously hurt from an auto accident. Your dad will be here in the morning."

Billy and I rushed to the hospital for the first of many hours of visiting. Steve, who lay unconscious with a skull fracture, was unaware of our visits. It was there, too, I finally met the boy who was to have been my date, now harnessed into an impossible assemblage of pulleys and wires for his many broken bones.

Two more weeks passed with Steve much the same. On my

Another Day, Another Miracle

way home to our boarding house, I stopped a moment to listen
to the sound of the carillon at Perkin's Blind Institute as the
blind played mother's favorite hymn, "Jesus Calls Us O'er the
Tumult." Still shaken by the fading notes, I hurried home
where I found a letter waiting from Rick. Scanning his bold
writing, blurred words hit me, "Perhaps our friendship is a
mistake. We don't seem to have lighthearted fun anymore. . . .
See you around."

I read it again, still unbelieving. First mother, then Steve, and
now Rick. "O God, aren't you tired of battering me?" I protested. I moved out into the rainy night. Maybe walking would
help the suffocating feeling in my chest. Of course Rick didn't
care for me with my darned stockings, shabby coat, and luster-
less hair. How could he, or anyone else for that matter? Add to
that my grades plummeting, my inadequacy at mothering Billy,
and the picture of Steve's white face on the pillow. . . . "Oh,
mother, where is your God now?" I cried out. "I once thought
God wanted me to follow him, but where? He took you away
just when I needed you most. What kind of love and protection
is this?"

Without realizing it my steps had turned away from the
Charles River road back toward our old house on the other side
of the railroad tracks. I approached the railroad overpass.
Metal clanked under my feet. As my hand slid along the railing,
it felt cold and damp under desperate fingers. Far in the distance
below, two yellow discs glowed vaguely, an approaching train.
It seemed suspended in time.

It drew closer, the lights like foggy eyes drawing me. My
body pressed against the railing; I gasped between shuddering
sobs. I jumped at an eerie whistle, felt the bridge begin to
vibrate. It could all be over in a minute, no more worries. Now,
I thought. Now . . .

Just then I heard footsteps at the far end of the bridge. Oh, no,
I mustn't be seen like this. I brushed my wet face with my coat
sleeve. The train roared beneath us. Like a statue I froze as
steps drew nearer. I half-turned toward a couple approaching,
silhouetted by a street light behind them. Even as I started in
recognition, a voice called, "Why, isn't that Ceil?"

42

How could it be? But it was—Paul and Marian Evans, our church youth counselors who lived far on the other side of town. But why were they here and at this time?

Marian's arm was warm around my shoulder. "How wonderful running into you like this. We tried to call you all afternoon. You must have stayed late at college. We've missed you at church lately. But what we really called about was to ask you to be Martha in the Easter pageant. Will you do it?"

I don't recall what I answered. I only remember looking into the kind eyes of these friends and comprehending that somehow God had sent them out of the mist when I most needed someone to help me. God must care a little, I thought.

A few nights later, I had another wonderful experience, something that I hugged to me and never told before this. At almost-sleeping time, it seemed as if a presence with the radiance and feel of mother stood by my bed, leaned over, kissed my cheek lightly, and said, "Darling, everything will be all right. Don't grieve for me anymore. I am with God. I love you dearly." Just as suddenly the room was empty, but a warmth was still on my cheek even after the haunting dream had vanished from view.

As my remembrance of that dream of mother faded out, I became aware of the girls around me, of tears swimming in Annie's beautiful eyes, and of my need for a good blow.

"Heavens," I said, "here I go taking up the whole Bible study lesson with my personal stories."

"Isn't that what we're here for?" Marge countered. "To learn about God's Word and what he does in people's lives?"

Since the time was late, the group broke up quickly, but I sensed a tenderness and was glad I had told about God's visitation. It's difficult to share an experience which you fear will be unbelievable to others. But I found then that where a group gathers in faith, it is easier to open locked doors of the heart.

As I walked to the car, it suddenly hit me. This was exactly what Madame Chiang Kai-shek had described in her book, *The Sure Victory*[1] Her little prayer group of women found courage to tell how God not only sustained them in trouble, but gave them victory.

Another Day, Another Miracle

My unburdening opened the way for others. A week later, Marge shared with us that she was finding little strength from her church and that her husband, a doctor, had no interest in the whole religious bit. As the weeks passed, Marge's tension increased, her eyes darkened with pain. Long a chain-smoker, she told us that the more she studied God's Word, the more she felt compelled to stop. She came less often. When she did, she seemed like a rigid island, withdrawn, seldom joining in—unlike her old self.

None of us will forget the day Vera opened the floodgates for all of us. It wouldn't have hit us so hard if she hadn't been one of our most devout Christians. Even before a Bible opened, she blurted, "Girls, I need your prayers." Her mouth crumpled, tears slid down her face. We began praying silently for her. With an effort her husky voice began, "It's our daughter. . . . She's been sneaking out at night. We've tried everything—warnings, denial of privileges, but nothing stops her. She's seeing some sailor, but she clams up when we question her. I'm terribly worried." Evelyn handed her a tissue while we waited for her sobs to ease. We had heard something of problems with her adopted daughter, but never dreamed Vera and her husband wouldn't be able to handle them.

Marge leaned toward Vera, her face also wet with tears. "I never dreamed you had problems, too. Mine seemed enormous, but not against yours. Dear Vera, we'll pray for you and your daughter. It's funny, but you helped me solve my problem just now. I've got to stop trying to make my husband over into the Christian image. Looks like my job is to work on myself and let God work on Bob."

We all stared at Marge. How different she looked, her tension gone, her face softened with tears for another. She reminded me of the change that takes place in a stone submerged in water. Its hardness wavers into softness, and new color emerges.

Before I knew it, I was telling about the awful day when our daughter, in her teens, was late coming home. When she finally phoned, her voice sounded like someone else. "Mother, I've left home."

"Home?" I echoed. "Where are you?"

"At Carolyn's. If you want me back, you'll have to let me do as I please."

This couldn't be. We hadn't even had an argument. I just couldn't believe this was our Gail, and more than anything I wanted to say, "Come home on any terms, just come home," but I didn't, thank God. Somehow I said, "Darling, we love you more than anything in this world, but, as parents, we must do what we feel is right. I pray with all my heart that you'll want to come home." The phone clicked off before I could say more. I stood there numbly bitting my lip, finally aware of our aged black cleaning woman who looked toward me, the wisdom of centuries in her kind eyes.

"Honey, all fifteen-year-olds goes through that running away thing. She's just testin' you. Wait and see."

Sure enough, half an hour later, Gail was home. She rushed up to her room with a sheepish look and the subject was never brought up again.

Vera's outburst had been a catharsis for all of us to unburden our defeats, to open pride-shut heart chambers. We felt close as never before. For at least two it became a turning point. Vera arranged a small wedding, anticipated the coming birth of a grandchild.

To Marge's surprise, she not only won the battle against cigarettes, but the greater one of peace within her marriage. Her once-frozen face turned radiant as she told of her son's new-found relationship with Christ, brought about through an organization called Young Life which meets in neighborhood homes. Even more surprising, her husband encouraged the sardine-like filling of their home with kids "turned on for Jesus."

Even the tragedy, later that winter, of her husband's accident while attempting to extract a light bulb from its kitchen socket, turned out for good, as God promises. With a tourniquet Marge's husband saved his lifeblood, but tendons in his wrist and fingers were seriously injured. The fingers in that hand were rigid. For a doctor that seemed disastrous.

Through trying days and months, Marge served both as driver and substitute fingers for her husband. To her joy, she

45

found him turning little by little to God for help. Finally, the scientist allowed the Man of Galilee to penetrate his life.

There were also others changed by prayer and God's Word. An alcoholic couple with two children found some measure of victory over alcohol through the help of a university psychological team, but their greatest help came when they found Christ themselves. Now both write and produce films for schools in which their new life in Christ is reflected.

I discovered that interdenominational Bible study groups are common today. Eleanor Searle Whitney of the Vanderbilt millions started one in her affluent Long Island community that was laughingly referred to as the "Cadillac Bible study set."

You don't have to be a Bible scholar to start such a group. A Minnesota women's state golf champion stated before a large group of women, "I was scared to death when I started our Bible group, literally just one chapter ahead of the women myself. But I found the courage when we got hung up on a passage to suggest we ask an authority and discuss the answer at our next meeting." Many guide books are designed just for beginner neighborhood groups. Actually God does much of the answering when groups study his Word. Wise leaders dwell on the centrality of Christ, not on differences such as baptism and Communion.

Madame Chiang Kai-shek tells of a desperately unhappy woman who joined her Bible study group after losing her whole family of six children. Every one of the thousand-odd aboard a ship from Formosa drowned, including the woman's last surviving son. "The mother almost lost her mind. She would not believe her boy was really dead. She stood on the wharf for three days and nights as each ship came in, her eyes straining at the face of every soldier filing down the gangplank from the ships. She kept asking, 'Do you know a man by the name of Yeh I-kun? Was he in your outfit?' When the last ship was unloaded, she gazed for a long time at the unfeeling ocean which had taken her child. Returning home, she tried to kill herself. Nothing would comfort her. She sat with a vacuous stare, huddled in silence. When this woman was brought to our meeting, we all showed her our concern and sympathy. We prayed with her that

God would comfort and sustain all whose hearts were breaking through bereavement. Some wept with her. . . .

"To our amazement," Madame Chiang Kai-shek continues, "she returned voluntarily without urging. Her mind cleared. Within a year after she joined the group, she was baptized. It is not often that one hears prayers so powerful, so beautiful, and so filled with God's grace as hers."[2]

Madame Chiang Kai-shek urges a chain of prayer groups around the world; a turning to God of all those who call themselves Christians and who will welcome amongst them those who have no spiritual home.

As churches become highly organized there is often little chance for sharing personal problems together. Even the piousness of most churches makes it harder for Christians to share their personal failures with church members. A truly Christ-centered Bible study can break down such barriers.

FIVE **Partnership in a Love Business**

If Simmons College had decided to give an award to the student least likely to succeed in business, I would have received that award. Not only was my shorthand jerky and indecipherable, but my typing inevitably resembled an eraser scrub-out. I can only believe that Simmons relaxed when I married immediately after college. Now their business dropout wouldn't disgrace them.

Who would have believed that twenty-five years later, the girl who had nightmares about typewriters was voluntarily attending a School of Christian Writing sponsored by *Decision* magazine? I enrolled, not because I had any idea God could make a writer out of me, but simply because I had become a new Christian and wanted to tell the world about it. The pen seemed a mighty tool to do just that even if it did involve a typewriter for the final draft.

The first afternoon we were taken on a tour. I made mental notes of a soundproof area for computers, a warehouse bustling with the largest mailing business in the Twin Cities, acres of desks, and employees used to working while tourists filed past; followed by artwork and layouts as though we were in Greenwich Village, only all designed around the person of Christ. Our attractive guide stopped at the entrance to the business office. "This office is extremely important," she stated. "Here decisions are made concerning the Lord's money. Since

49

it is the people's love gift, not a penny must be wasted."

I studied her face to see if she was kidding. Never before in my life as the wife of a sales manager had I heard business talk in terms of accounting to the Lord. Still no one could doubt her sincerity. She meant it. And why not? I thought. Even the elevator boy this morning had talked to us about how Jesus had changed him from gutter-gangster to elevator boy in a Christian business.

I looked at those around me: missionaries, editors, a speech writer for the astronauts, ministers, gangling young men, and tottering elderly women. Where did I, a housewife who had never written anything but letters to the editor, fit into this crowd? I tried to look spiritually intelligent (however you do that). But the mask soon fell off when I discovered that no one there cared who I was. Instead, they were concerned with my relationship to God and my skill in writing about him.

We studied the power of words aptly used as opposed to clichés. We were inspired by theologians; encouraged by news-papermen, novelists, and publishers. The spirit of love, intangible but real, soon made me forget that I came alone. They cared as much about helping the beginner as about stimulating the veteran writer. Later in the afternoon, at a park picnic, Dr. Sherwood Wirt, editor of *Decision* magazine, discussed our manuscripts with us personally.

By evening I felt I would explode as ideas swirled in my head. The time for the banquet came all too soon, ending our three days together. God must really mean me to write, I thought, when I found myself seated next to Catharine Brandt, a polished short-story writer. It was Catharine with her gentle graciousness who later steered me into the Minnesota Christian Writers' Guild, encouraged me to take an Oklahoma University extension course, and gave me lists of books on writing.

Some time later, I again met the young man of the elevator at a writers' group where he shared his life story. From my place across the table from him, I felt nervous currents that made his fingers clench and his eyes dart around the room. Moments later, he told of swinging chains from one side of the street to another, destroying cars. I was repelled.

Wasn't I supposed to write of beautiful experiences, not of ugliness and devastation?

He continued on to tell of arrests, correctional institutions, and, finally, of an experience at a Life Line camp. I could hardly believe the change in his face as he told simply and quietly of Christ's turning out his hate and replacing it with love so that he could return to his neighborhood and work with troubled kids. The tension in him uncoiled. A gentle peace took its place as he talked of Jesus. If God could transform latent raw anger into purity as I had seen in the face of that young man, I knew I had to write his story. That became my first published manuscript, "Me Third," for Harvest Publications.[1]

But God had further plans for me besides writing and evangelizing—the promotion of a film. At the School of Christian Writing, we were invited to see a preview of the film *The Restless Ones,* created by World Wide Pictures, a part of the Billy Graham Evangelistic Association. As the pictures flicked by, I watched with horror the desecration of a church altar, racing motorcycles, a girl trapped hopelessly by her alcoholic mother, young love hurt, a family rooted into material ties, revolt, anger. I became the film mother torn apart by youth's problems. My face was still wet as the lights flashed on. This was real, like the world all around me, and the answer lay, as the film made plain, in a personal relationship to Jesus Christ.

I wanted every young person to see that film, to see himself in relationship to God's plans for him. But how? The question gnawed at me. What could I say or do about it? I longed to be able to buy a ticket for every teen-ager in the city, but we were having to watch our budget more carefully these days.

On my return home, my husband listened patiently to my outpourings. However, when he realized the potential power of *The Restless Ones* to influence youth toward God, his enthusiasm matched mine. "Maybe we could take some kids to see it," he mused.

"Not just church kids," I added, "slum kids and rich unchurched kids too. It ought to be a happening. How about a date night: dinner and theater?"

"Yes, they might go for that. But it can't be expensive, and it ought to be food the kids like. How about a smörgasbord where they can choose what they like?"

"That just might work." We were off as the idea picked up momentum.

Several days later, Hugh and I sat nervously in Ken Bliss's impressive office at World Wide Pictures. We were prepared to plunge. "We'd like to take 100 tickets to *The Restless Ones,*" Hugh stated boldly as though we were agents for Metro Goldwyn Mayer. That represented $100, no small amount to us.

"You see," Hugh blurted, enthusiasm overcoming caution, "we plan a teen dinner-theater smörgasbord at a Sveden House restaurant and bus to the Orpheum Theater for $1.50 and the film at $1.00 or a package deal of $2.50. We've only lived here a few months, but if you'll give us yard signs and posters, we figure God will supply the kids and the people to help us promote the idea."

Ken listened, a surprised twinkle in his blue eyes. As the plan began to take shape, Ken's enthusiasm matched ours. Hugh reached for the hundred tickets. "Why don't you take one thousand tickets?" Ken suggested. "If they don't sell, you can bring them back. This thing could really grow."

I gasped, but my husband dreams big. He reached for the thousand tickets. All the way home, I clutched the box, wondering if anyone had ever been robbed of one thousand dollars in tickets to a Billy Graham film.

There were many times in the days ahead when I was overcome with doubts. How could anyone who knew less than thirty young people in a strange city sell one thousand tickets? How could I, who still added on my fingers, keep records for a venture of this size?

But God was in charge. The more we stepped out into the unknown, the more he sent in reinforcements. Everywhere we went, we met God's militia. Our assistant pastor lined up seminarians from Bethel College who were already school bus drivers, to cover transportation. Men whom Hugh met through Christian Business Men's Club signed up as area chairmen to contact local churches of every denomination. A CPA from our church took the books from my trembling fingers; an eye surgeon, a new Christian himself because of the recent office call of a Campus Crusader, contacted doctors and dentists and helped us organize. Our dear Catholic neighbor, after seeing a preview of the film, lined up priests and community leaders from her diocese.

Though we were getting support from evangelical groups, few ticket orders came in from churches belonging to the National Council of Churches. At about this time, we met a dynamic and talented young man, Rev. Emery Barrette, then chaplain of the Saint Paul Juvenile Court and later to be a candidate for Congress. He, too, caught the spark. Wherever he spoke, stressing this film's ability to bridge communication lines between teens and their parents, churches in the more liberal tradition called in for tickets.

Young people became ticket sellers in their school choirs and other groups. Tables set up at shopping areas showed sample scenes with sound from the film, while attractive girls sold tickets. Posters and yard signs dotted suburbs. Sponsors were found for kids in ghetto neighborhoods.

Finally the long anticipated day arrived. Over a thousand kids dined at three Sveden Houses. Then, they were bused with blasting police sirens to the Orpheum Theater where five hundred more joined them to see *The Restless Ones*. We learned later that it was the largest organized group in the nation to see it. Lives were changed. At the conclusion of the film, back in the wings of the theater, I prayed with some young people, saw their eyes fill with tears, tears of joy and hope.

God was aware of what happened for he planned it all when he planned a writing career and an evangelistic message for me back at the School of Christian Writing.

Even as Christ said, "I must be about my Father's business" (Luke 2:49), I have had the joy of serving in a small way in God's business, just by being available when he nudges me to live dangerously for him.

SIX **Tears in the Soup**

I prefer to wake to a lark's call than to a rooster's crow. No swift tumble from bed nor swish of cold water for me. Instead, I like to curl deep into my down pillow as long as possible, then move like a sleepwalker into the kitchen. I set the table to the rhythm of Hugh's shower song. Breakfast is usually the brightest moment of the day for us, full of chatter and sharp appetite. The day's adventures are laid out. All too soon my men are gone and the house dons a quiet mantle.

My day unfolds luxuriously as I tuck myself back into a still-warm bed, sip coffee, and spread out the state of the land in crisp newspaper headlines.

But no such state of euphoria was to take place that blustery November morning. Wet snow thumped against our bedroom window panes. "Where are my boots?" my husband yelled. Meanwhile, I could hear the grinding of the starter on young Hugh's iced car. As I yanked assorted boots from a hamper under the stairs, I heard Hugh, Sr. mumble something about a lost shovel. I watched him stash a heavy garden spade into the back seat of the car.

"What in the world is that for?" I protested, eyes wide open for once.

"You never know how deep the snow will be in Duluth," he muttered. "By the way, honey, I'll stay overnight there in weather like this."

He was gone before I could file countercharges like, "Hey, you didn't shovel the front porch" or, more important, "How will I get to my girls' missionary class tonight through the deepening snow?"

This day I ignored the morning paper's display of snow-blocked highways, too concerned with my day's problems to worry about Hugh's. Instead I started simmering a soup bone, my favorite prescription for a stormy day.

Strange, isn't it, I thought, how the queasy smell of grayish beef bone finally blends into delicious goodness with the addition of vegetables. I selected a large onion. My eyes smarted, tears spurted as I diced onion bits into the bubbling soup. Plows continued to scrape outside. Snow plopped steadily against the house as wind picked up. Clearly it was a bad storm and it looked as though I was to be a prisoner. My own "sorry-for-me" tears joined onion tears to mingle in the steaming kettle.

While I stirred in tomato sauce, expectant faces from my missionary guild girls seemed to stare at me through the misty steam. One, half lost in a wool-tassled cap, pleaded, "What about me? I'm your shy mouse. You wanted to bring me out, remember?"

Another face moved in, the new girl whose haunting gypsy eyes dominated a delicate bone structure. "It's rough to move to the city from a farm," she seemed to say. "I love God, but kids, ugh, what cliques, and the worst seem to be in churches."

They had problems and so did I. No one but my family knew about my helplessness in deep snow, a leftover from my spinal fusion. In Indiana I could manage the usual half-inch that fell, though I always knew I couldn't get up alone if I should stumble. But then God never let me fall all those times I drove alone to meetings. How I treasured those benediction words, "Unto him that is able to keep you from falling, and to present you faultless" (Jude 24). Oh, yes, how good God was in not letting me slip for two whole years, but now my needs were different.

"Yes, God," I muttered. "You kept your promise all those months when I couldn't get up without help. You kept me from falling, and I'm grateful, but this is different. You know these muscles won't lift my left leg over deep snow.

"Is it really important to you that I teach these teen-agers? I suppose they are small potatoes when you are running a whole kingdom. But to me it's important, and I think it is to them. And now that you've taken my husband out of town, how do you expect me to get out to the kids?"

More tears splashed into the soup. I stirred mechanically as the faces faded and misery closed in on the soup and me.

"Well, God, if you don't plan to just stash me in a rocking chair all winter, you'll have to do something about my leg. It's up to you now. I give up."

The soup simmered on and a hasty glance at the clock warned me it was either shower time—or skip it. Within seconds I was in the bathroom, undressed, and already lifting my damaged leg with my hand over the tub edge. Warm water soothed my shoulder blades. I soaped one arm, transferred soap to the other. As happened so often when I was in a hurry, the pesky soap slipped to the tub, seeming to grin whitely back. Usually when this happened in the narrow confines of the tub, I was unable to bend and retrieve it, a chore I left for my menfolks later. Without reaching for another, lined up on the tub edge, I stooped and picked up the fallen bar, and continued the sudsing process. Halfway through a thought hit me. You bent down. Something let you bend, I puzzled. Could God have loosened those muscles? Only God could do that. In wonder I flexed my leg. Could it be? It must be! Tears of exaltation mingled with shower drops. "Oh, God, what is happening?"

Now bursting with excitement, I turned off the water, stepped to the bath mats. Only then did I realize my left leg had lifted over the tub edge by itself without my even willing it. Draped in a towel, I rushed to our bedroom where I started dressing, laughing through tears like a child.

"I can't believe it. I just can't believe it," I chattered. "Maybe I'm crazy." But another phenomenon convinced me something real had happened. Ordinarily I had to toss my stocking over the toe of my left foot since I couldn't bend my leg up close enough to ease it on. But this time I could bend my knee enough to slide my toes into the stocking just like anyone else.

God had healed my leg enough for me to lift it over snow. Bits of Bible verses hung in the air. "My God shall supply all your need" (Phil. 4:19), he said and also, "Ask and it shall be given you" (Matt. 7:7).

God knew my need and he answered it. He must feel teaching teen-agers is important enough to heal a woman's leg. Now I wondered why I hadn't asked him to heal me years ago. But then, perhaps this was the first time I needed my leg to be about *his* business."

I also knew that if I had never read of God's answer to Catherine Marshall when she was ill with tuberculosis and prayed for help,[1] I would never have had the nerve to ask God for healing. I'd have agreed with others who say, "Sure, way back then, Christ healed the sick and taught his disciples to heal, but this is the twentieth century. Doctors do whatever healing is done today."

God showed me another time that he cares about the little things. If a miracle were to take place, I always thought it would be something big like healing the blind or the helpless paralytic. Perhaps the Bible gives us this impression with its dramatic incidents, but I found the God who knows how many hairs we have on our heads cares about the tiny problems, too.

Some eight months later, on a July evening, I wiped my hot forehead. It was an effort to pack my overnight case. My throat was sore. Swallowing was an effort. I longed to climb into bed and ignore everything. But I was committed to join thirty church teen-agers for a three-day weekend at our friends' cabin at Cross Lake, Minnesota.

Louise and I had the food all planned. Boxes of buns, ketchup, and cereal weighted down the rear of our car. How could Louise cook and chaperone that bunch without help? It wasn't fair to her. By this time I was used to sharing all problems with God, not just emergencies. After all, he had demonstrated he could solve big problems. I wondered how he was on the little ones.

"How about this, God?" I began. "In good faith, I agreed to help with this gang and you know there are kids in this crowd with real hangups. Maybe they can be reached in a place that combines waterskiing with birch grove meditation. If you think

I'm needed and that this is important to youth, please do something about my throat. I'm not much good to anybody as it is. It's OK if my throat is sore all next week. Please just heal it for tomorrow morning.''

To my amazement, I woke with a pain-free throat. God asks us to pray believing. I did and he answered. Why is it we're always so shocked when the seemingly impossible happens? He has even given us the answer to that, ''For with God nothing shall be impossible'' (Luke 1:37).

As I shared God's wonderful healing with my family, my son grinned. ''That's great, Mom, but I sure feel sorry for you when God sends back the sore throat next week. It could be a 'beaut.' ''

So much for God's healing of oneself. Perhaps it is hard for us to believe God will heal others unless we have experienced this mystery. At any rate, I was eager that all might know and claim healing through him. I was to find him sufficient for all in my hospital adventures as a ''pink lady,'' but only when I prayed the prayer of commitment. That is, if before arriving, I prepared the way by talking with God, requesting, ''If there is some one at the hospital with a need, fill me with your Spirit, and help me answer that need in your way.''

Early one January morning as I peered through an iced windshield on my way to Midway Hospital in Saint Paul, Minnesota, where I would take patients by wheelchair to physical therapy, I thought, ''Just anyone could do this kind of volunteer work. Is there any Christian opportunity in it?''

On my way down the corridor after signing in, I wondered again if today I might meet Miss Nelson, a retired teacher from Bethel College, who was feeling the discouragement of prolonged illness. Although I'd been praying over two months for her, I hadn't yet met her. So far, a therapist treated her privately in her room.

At 10:30 a therapist signaled me. ''You can go up with Gregg (our orderly) to get Mrs. Nelson in room 264. You'll need to get extra help on the floor.''

Mrs. Nelson, great! I'd finally meet her. But what on earth could I say to cheer her?

Another Day, Another Miracle

Three nurses joined us at Mrs. Nelson's bedside, each holding an edge of her bath blanket, to swing her onto the stretcher. A large woman whose crumpled features were dominated by dark, sunken eyes, she could move only her head and arms.

As we struggled, she moaned in pain, a tear trembling down her cheek. "Oh, I'm such a lot of trouble to you," she said. "If only I could help you more."

Looking into her pleading eyes, I blurted, "Mrs. Nelson, don't feel bad. Four years ago, after I had spinal surgery, it took six to lift me and here I am to help you."

Her eyes widened as she whispered, "Can that be?"

"Yes, my dear, it's not only so, but I'm thankful for that time. It was the beginning of my search for Christ."

Suddenly I became aware that the three nurses, the orderly, and the other patient in the room were listening intently. At the same moment it hit me that this wasn't the Christian Miss Nelson, but someone else. I blushed at my stupidity, but the new Mrs. Nelson reached for my hand and started a barrage of questions. By now she was secure on the stretcher. With Gregg at one end, we propelled her along the quiet corridor to the basement.

As we walked, I learned that her husband was in critical condition, under the care of 'round-the-clock nurses. She was unable to go to him because of intense pain from arthritis, an internal bleeding ulcer, and ulcerous sores on her legs.

Meanwhile, she learned how I found Christ after a desperate search.

Back in the therapy room our aide, Peggy, and I lowered Mrs. Nelson into the water in a large Hubbard tank while the talk flowed on. She was still holding my hand. As I left to care for another patient, I squeezed her hand, murmuring that I would pray constantly for her and for her dear sick husband.

And so I did—without ceasing. All week her eyes and her need haunted me.

One week later when I walked back into the large therapy room, a woman sat comfortably in a wheelchair chatting to our therapist, Fred. As she turned, I was amazed to discover it was my Mrs. Nelson, her eyes alive and sparkling, her body moving easily, looking ten years younger.

As our eyes met, she called out, "Here's my friend who prayed for me. Just look at me now. Isn't it wonderful? My ulcer is almost healed, I can move freely, and, as if that weren't enough of a miracle, my husband is also much better. Oh, my dear, how can I ever thank you enough for your prayers? How good God is to me!"

I stood transfixed as the other therapists gathered around the glowing woman. There was no doubt that God had been at work. I marveled that he had used my prayer for one Miss Nelson to lead me to another who needed him more. God can turn a case of mistaken identity into his marvelous plan.

Just one week later as Mr. and Mrs. Nelson waited to be wheeled to an approaching car, homeward bound, she smiled as she said, "Don't you feel sorry for all those who don't really know God?"[2]

Still another cold morning, this time in November, I again prayed the prayer of commitment, but that morning at Midway Hospital passed without incident. As the X ray department began to empty for lunch, I carried down a small blond boy in nursery-patterned flannel pajamas. His only response to cuddling was a thin wail. He looked about three, but was too thin and pale for me to be sure. A medical technician placed him on a table in a room dominated by a large machine called a scanner. She explained that the small light of the machine's arm as it passed slowly over the child's chest and abdomen indicated on a chart to the right of the machine a pattern which helped physicians diagnose hard-to-detect cancers, such as malignant tumors in the liver area.

The X ray lounge emptied as patients and employees left for lunch. I thumbed through an outdated magazine as I waited impatiently for one o'clock and lunch. Heavy footsteps broke the silence. I heard whispers, then muffled sobs that seemed to come from the corridor near the child's room. As I peered around the partition, three desolate figures waited by the door. One, a young woman, left her seat at a nurse's call. Feeling rather like an intruder, I sat down next to the elderly couple. "Is there anything I can do for you . . . perhaps a cup of coffee?" I asked.

The grandmother looked up in surprise. "No, thanks," she sighed, then motioned, "That's our little grandson in there. He's terribly sick with a big tumor. Now the doctors fear it's affected his liver and nothing much can be done." She paused to blow her nose. "He's such a dear . . . so good, too." Then addressing a gaunt man on her right, "This is my husband. He really should be home. Last week I was here in this hospital to see him, but he wanted to be with us when we found out about Jerry. Seems like trouble sort of stacks up sometimes." She mopped her eyes, glanced anxiously toward her husband.

"I carried your grandson down about an hour ago," I began. "He is a dear. I'm sorry he's so ill. But sometimes when the doctors give up, God takes over. I belong to a Christian women's prayer chain. Would you like us to pray for your grandson?"

Her eyes widened, "Would you?"

"We certainly will," I smiled back.

Just then the young mother appeared, her blue eyes blurred with tears. "Come on," she whispered.

They were gone. At the technician's request, I went in to sit by the sleeping child. The machine's light beam continued to move inexorably back and forth across the child's fragile chest, mapping out the troubled area. As I followed the narrow beam in the darkened room Christ's words were repeated over and over in my mind, "I am the way, the truth, and the life; no man cometh unto the Father, but by me" (John 14:6). Christ's light is a thousand times more powerful than the light of this expensive machine made by man.

Later as I hurried down the crowded central hospital corridor, I met the child's relatives returning from the coffee shop. The grandmother reached for my hand. "This is the lady who promised to pray for Jerry," she explained to her daughter. The girl stared at me blankly. Anyone could see that her mind and heart were back with her child.

We did pray and I often thought of that heartbroken little group. It wasn't until six weeks later that I learned what happened. A slip of paper fell from an early Christmas card. The scratchy writing read, "I had to write to you to tell you of our joy this Christmas. A miracle has happened. Our son Jerry is completely healed. The tumor seemed to vanish. The doctors were as astonished as we were and can't find any medical answer for it. But we know the answer. God healed him.

"How can I ever thank you and your prayer chain enough for this gift of our child's life? Please thank your friends for all of us."

I read it again—unbelievable medically, but God's answer to prayer for healing. I thanked him joyously and marveled again at the power for good that he promises and delivers when we pray, believing.

But then why should we be surprised? Long ago God delivered a promise to Moses that he keeps for us today. "If you will listen to the voice of the Lord your God, and obey it, and do what is right, then I will not make you suffer the diseases I send on the Egyptians: for I am the Lord who heals you" (Exod. 15:26, *The Living Bible*).

SEVEN Works of the Hands and the Spirit

When God renews and regenerates our spirit, he doesn't mean for the baby Christian to sit in some holy vacuum, removed from the world and its need. However, before God could use us for others, we needed to learn more of his plan for us both through his Word, Bible study groups, and Bible courses. My husband, Hugh, joined a luncheon group called Christian Business Men's Committee, International, as well as an early morning Bible study group. He frequently returned from these sessions frustrated because of his inability to understand a passage and confused with theological concepts beyond him. But he kept going. We comforted each other in our Bible ignorance. We also felt some anger that the church that should have been our teacher over the years had left us biblically handicapped. It was easier to fault the church than ourselves.

How comforting it is to know that God takes us kindergarten Christians of mature years without reproach, step by step in new knowledge even as we grow step by step in faith. We would have studied even harder if we had known God's future plans for us.

About this time I took a tour of Gillette Crippled Children's Hospital. As we approached a large ward, the tour leader explained, "We have some children here who, because of severe handicaps, spend months and sometimes years with us. Many have no visitors at all.

"Can you imagine," she continued, "what it is like for a child to sit on his bed Sunday after Sunday watching parents and friends arrive bearing gifts while no one comes near his bed?"

"Is it because no one cares?" I asked, appalled.

"Sometimes, but more often because parents may live miles away with farms or businesses to take care of and simply are not able to afford either time or money to visit their child," she replied.

"Would it be possible for us to visit such children?" I asked.

"That is our hope," she smiled. "Several churches already bring visitors on a particular Sunday of the month to act as substitute family and friends to our lonely children."

Thus began a thrilling ministry. A small group from our church soon began our monthly treks to Gillette. Often our visiting group was made up largely of young people. They had a special talent for making the kids laugh, a zest in playing games.

Awakened one blustery March Sunday by our dog's barking at the paper boy, I used the time to pray what I call the Good Samaritan prayer, "Oh, dear Lord, if there is a child with a spiritual need or *any* kind of need, lead me to him and give me words to answer his need."

I dressed, fixed breakfast, and rushed off to church. After dinner we finally arrived at Gillette where the voice of our little Indian friend Bonita called toward me, "My mommy's here. Hello, mommy. Where's daddy?"

As I hurried to the Stryker frame where her small body lay flat, healing from spinal surgery, Bonita happily announced my visit to her friends in the adjoining beds. Many of them were already unwrapping gifts from their loving families. But Bonita had no gifts. No one came to see little ones like her until the hospital invited churches to select a Sunday to visit these children who usually had no visitors.

Bonita loves pocketbooks and knows mine well enough to find my little blue New Testament and to turn to the picture of the baby Jesus. We read and played games together, smiling at her giggling friends. One resembled a miniature adult in her neck brace. Another had a marbled mask from burns on one side of her face. It was soon time to go to the young boys' ward, but Bonita clung to my hand. She needed love badly. It was only months later when other visitors began befriending her that she stopped calling us mom and dad for she no longer needed to save face with the other children. As I left her, I promised to return and say good-bye.

The boys' beds had been moved around since we were last there. In seeking Brian, a favorite of mine, I encountered Mike. "Are you looking for a boy with one leg?" he called.

"Yes," I answered. He wanted to play a game called "war."

This can be a long venture. Bored with the game, I glanced around his bed. There on his night stand lay *Good News for Modern Man,* a modern language version of the New Testament.[1]

"Can you read that?" I asked surprised, noting the small body with one skinny leg crossed over an adjoining stump.

"Sure," his bright eyes signaled.

"I'll bet your dad is awfully proud of you, Mike." I smiled.

"My dad died in the war and my mommy didn't want me, so I have a foster mother."

"Do you remember your dad?" I asked, shocked that anyone could give up this bright, likable little fellow.

"Just a little," he added.

"Well, I'm sure your dad in heaven is proud of you. I know my husband would be proud of a son like you."

Mike pushed his leg over the bed, hunched toward me, his eyes two blue question marks of intensity.

"Tell me," he said, "what's it like in heaven? Will someone get me from a grave? What will I eat in heaven? Will there be houses in heaven?"

Asking God to help me, I answered as best I could. "Jesus said, 'In my Father's house are many mansions. . . . I go to prepare a place for you' (John 14:2). Mike, we can only guess that it will be more beautiful than any place here on earth."

"Does he have these mansions ready for us yet?" he questioned.

67

"Well, it's been two thousand years since Christ was here in person on earth. I'm sure everything is ready and waiting for us. Don't you think so, Mike?"

"Yes, I bet. But tell me, how strong is God? Can he lift the Empire State Building?"

This time I smiled into the intense blue eyes, "Oh, I'm sure he can lift the Empire State Building. After all, he made our whole world, didn't he?"

"Yes, I guess God's strong, but how do we know he can make *us* strong?"

"The only way I know is that it happened to me," I replied. I could see the puzzled look in his eyes. After all, I didn't look like a tower of strength. "One summer," I began, "I was to take thirty kids from our church to a Minnesota lake for a three-day weekend. The day before we were to leave, I came down with a bad sore throat, so sore I could hardly swallow. Since I knew I wouldn't be much good to the kids with this sore throat, I prayed to God. I said, 'Dear God, I need to be well enough to cook for these kids, watch them in water sports, and see that they get their rest. Please heal my throat for the weekend. If you want to bring it back Tuesday, that is all right.' And you know, Mike, when I woke up the next morning it was all gone."

"Wow!"

"That's what I mean by power. If you need strength to do something for others, God will send it to you."

As he mused quietly, I gathered up my things.

"Say, what'll we look like in heaven—if we don't eat and stuff? Will we look like angels, maybe?"

"Mike, I don't know, but you'll know your dad and he'll know you and best of all you'll see Christ."

"Can God talk?"

"I'm sure he can. Remember he said about his son Jesus, 'This is my beloved son.' And he talked to Moses."

"Did you know I'm having surgery Wednesday?" he blurted.

"No, I didn't. Will they operate on your leg?"

"They didn't tell me; just said I'm to be in special care on

Tuesday night. Say, would you come to see me there, would you?''

As I looked deep into his questioning eyes, I knew why he had wanted to know how strong God is. A little boy feels too weak to face things sometimes.

"I'll be there, Mike, if they'll let me. I'll be praying for you, too. God bless you."

I hurried out, watching his waving hand, with just time to say good-bye to Bonita as visiting hours ended.

God is strong enough to hold up the Empire State Building, but how will these little ones know it if no one ever tells them![2]

My calendar began to fill with visits to our new crippled children, Midway Hospital volunteer work as well as Midway Auxiliary presidential activities, Wednesday Bible study, plus a new luncheon group called Christian Women's Club. I was glad when June brought a slowdown of meetings even though each group to which I belonged revealed a new facet of God. Still, I needed time to think, feel, and write—time to enjoy my family.

Toward the end of June, a friend who worked as a nurse's aide at newly opened Lakeridge Nursing Home shared her concern with me. "I wish I had more time with the patients," she said wistfully. "There is nothing for most of them to do but watch TV or stare out the windows. Couldn't our church women do something about crafts or music, anything to give them a reason to look forward to the day."

"I'll talk to the girls," I promised. How really unfair it is, I thought, for some of us to be bogged down with activities while others sit with folded hands, their minds returning to happier days.

Our vacation plans soon dimmed this vision of the aged, but it continued to pop up unbidden over the summer months. Parchment faces with dulled eyes broke into my thoughts while I bounced in our boat over choppy water or gathered wild flowers for pressing. Even as I dodged God's nudges, their sunken eyes began to haunt me. "Why me?" I asked God. "You know what the stench of bedpans does to me, and you know how cranky and absentminded old people can be. I want to make lovely things. Don't send me there."

Another Day, Another Miracle

But I knew no peace until late in the summer when I conceded. "All right, Lord. No one else has volunteered. I know that some day I may be sitting all day staring into space with nobody caring. I'll go to them, but please, God, give me a joyous spirit or I won't do them a bit of good."

Not a bedpan did I see. Instead I watched gnarled hands spreading the petals of a burlap flower, tears of joy spilling over at a tender poem, shared laughter at a comic situation.

How well God sets the stage for his plans for us. He not only sent my friend Shirley to tell me of the loneliness at Lakeridge, but he sent Helen, a concert violinist and craft enthusiast to help work out a monthly crafts program there.

We met in a large sunny room with seventeen eager men and women. It was amazing what they could do in spite of their handicaps. A charming French lady threaded her needle just two inches from her nose, but quickly mastered making delicate loom straw flowers. Two stroke patients, a man and a woman with one good arm between them, worked as a team. One held a wire circle while the other tied felt bows for a Christmas wreath. Our February cherry trees leaned a bit, but the patients found them magnificent. How quickly the hour passed with busy hands and laughter. "My granddaughter will really like this," one said, while another could scarcely wait to take her fluffy Christmas tree to her seriously ill roommate.

Our laundry room at home began to overflow with spools, burlap, contact paper, and discards stored squirrel-like for future projects. Nothing we made will ever be exhibited in the Smithsonian Institution, but each of us needs to create a bit of something, and this they did—a tiny treasure to look at or to give away.

Meanwhile, seven women from Calvary Baptist Church planned and carried out monthly concerts, devotionals, and sometimes slide programs at Lakeridge Chapel, followed by homebaked cake or cookies shared with our new friends at coffee time. For four years, Thursday at 1:00 P.M. has been a special day at Lakeridge, a reason to put on a pretty dress, to tuck in a curler.

But as usually happens when one gives of oneself, all those in our circle of seven found ourselves attempting new ventures, like running projectors, giving travel lectures, baking with diabetics in mind, and in return God gave us deep beautiful friendships.

Few of our homes today are designed to accommodate elderly relatives. Nursing homes are an accepted way of life. Too, often, however, they are way stations to dying, though death may be postponed medically by drugs and tubes. Even this is not always a kindness to hopelessly ill sufferers.

What can Christians do to make the golden years meaningful? First, honor the elderly within the family circle. Oldsters want to be independent and useful as long as possible. Next, as their friends and family die, provide friendship, a link with the active world. Further still, little comforts take on importance. A friend of mine, Margaret Anderson, overheard a conversation between two white-haired ladies. "I don't know what I'll do when this dress falls apart. I can't find anything to fit me in the stores anymore," one said.

Her friend sighed, then added, "Me either. They just don't make them the same. I've given up on shopping."

Margaret took up the challenge and invited the ladies shopping the following day. She soon recognized their problem. Over the years their "cargo" had shifted, shoulders hunched over and stomach bunched forward. No wonder they looked odd in the new dresses. With her offer to alter them, each delightedly brought three dresses. They now feel and look elegant because someone cared enough to make adjustments.

In Fargo, North Dakota a young man whose crippled body necessitated his living in a nursing home, felt frustrated because he was contributing nothing to society. An understanding Lutheran pastor arranged for him to do odd office jobs at the church across the street two days a week as a volunteer. As a result the young man propels his wheelchair across winter's icy streets or summer's sweltering pavement as eagerly as any businessman.

We speak bitterly of the imprisoning of people in iron curtain countries, but are our handicapped and aged as free to live meaningful lives as we might make them?

As long as there are two-car families but no one to drive the lame to work, as long as we have free libraries of books but no one to read to the blind, as long as we drive past the homes of solitary aged who may fall and lie helpless for days, Christ's words might never have been spoken: "Inasmuch as ye have done it unto one of the least of these my brethren, ye have done it unto me" (Matt. 25:40).

EIGHT **Room in the Inn**

Six years ago our spacious four-bedroom Indiana home was occupied only by properly invited guests. Today our cramped saltbox in Minnesota has a tiny bedroom with yellow sheets freshly laid for God's guests.

Our home became an inn only after my husband, our son, and I yielded our lives to the urgent power of Christ. Since then, he does the inviting.

The first wayfarer was an elderly crippled woman, Florence. I met her at a New Neighbors Tea where she sat huddled away from the chattering ladies. Her story matched her desperate eyes—old, unwanted by her daughter, suicide-tempted.

On her visits to our roadside inn, it was exciting to hear her laugh, to watch her puzzle over Bible passages, and to sense the tug between Christ's values and her love for her remaining personal possessions.

I can still hear the click of her crutches as she zigzagged on them to the church front to receive Christ. We'll probably never know who is winning the tug-of-war between her possessions and Christ's way; but we do know she watches from her lonely window for God to come take her home—not the "drug overdose" way, but the "many mansion" way.

Our next guest came through an urgent phone call, a young woman from Rochester who had been a sort of baby sitter-housekeeper for a family. Her tearful voice told a story of attempted rape by the father of the house. Wondering how such things could happen, we arranged for her to occupy our little bedroom. Her pinched white face with its ragged hairline made her look older than her nineteen years.

It was only as she felt the peace and love of Christ that she relaxed and told us of her missionary years as a girl in Brazil. How wonderful to see her rigid cheeks flush with excitement and her darting frozen eyes change to brightness as she discussed happier days on the mission field.

By the week's end a job was waiting and a new home ready for our traveler where she could help a physically handicapped woman. God will not leave us comfortless, he tells us—nor does he.

Our most recent traveler also came to us by phone call. At 9:30 A.M. a faint voice said, "This is Val. You'll never guess where I am . . . at Saint Paul Ramsey County Hospital."

Puzzled, we looked at the lunch on the counter for a fishing trip with Val and her husband, Dale. We had enjoyed dinner at their apartment just the night before.

Her voice continued, "Last night after you left, we drove our other guest home. On our return we were hit by a freight train."

Rushing to the hospital, we scarcely knew our vibrant hostess of the previous evening. Her arms, legs, and body were purple with bruises; a head injury throbbed; a bloodsoaked bandage covered a broken artery on her right arm; but most of all she suffered pain in her right leg and knee.

We visited her husband briefly, the eighteen-inch cut on his head and his neck injury making him too ill for conversation.

On the way home we discussed the strangeness of my first meeting with Val. Through my confusion, but God's planning, I had attended what I thought was a New Neighbors meeting, but what turned out to be a Newcomers Club. Val was the hostess, outgoing, cheerful, friendly. As I sat uncomfortably on a high bar stool, I wondered what in the world I was doing there.

Our friendship developed over Christian Women's Club luncheons and Bible verses. We learned that an unfortunate church incident had soured Val's husband on the church route, while her family left the Catholic church because of antagonism toward the practice of confession.

After four days in the hospital, Val, still in extreme pain, came home with us. Tucked into yellow sheets, she snuggled down, her gratitude a shining light. As the pain grew worse, she turned more and more to a borrowed Bible. While reading the book of John, she asked many questions.

"For the first time I know what sin is," she flashed. "It's turning away from God. I always thought I didn't sin because I was good, but this is something different."

Our talks whirled around heavenly subjects, while our hands twisted Swiss straw into gay flowers. It was a week for Val in which spiritual joy mingled with physical pain.

One week later, a hospital checkup uncovered a fractured kneecap, accounting for the agonizing pain. She was rehospitalized, this time eased from pain by fluid drainage and finally a plaster leg cast.

For a week in our home we explored into God's kingdom, so new in God's way that we could only share the small truths we had found. But the light was shining in Val's pain-wracked eyes as she plotted a new course for her life.

This was one more in a series of experiences in which I was glad we had room in our inn.[1]

Just as a home can be a retreat to restore the spirit of battered people, so should our churches be places of comfort and restoration as well as meeting places with God. Ancient churches provided this mission, often equipped with huge kitchens and sleeping cubicles. Today, we tend to let welfare and the Salvation Army provide for such needs. Sadly enough many of today's churches have been accused of resembling country clubs far more than retreats for the homeless, sick, and lonely.

Even as the innkeeper of Bethlehem once deprived the expectant mother of God's Son of a needed place of rest, just so, long flights of steps with heavy doors too often keep handicapped people from worshiping at the church of their choice. Or again, a divorcée who receives a knife-edge glance when she sits in a pew next to a family man, senses no welcome in God's house. God looks on the heart. However, too many pew sitters may give the impression that no one should enter a sanctuary without haircut, bath, proper dress, and the appropriate skin color. It is perhaps ironic to call such a room a sanctuary!

Few intend the church to keep out the indigent, helpless, or lonely. It just seems to happen.

One young father in Cleveland, Ohio, found a way to open his church doors to those in the poor Hough district whose idea of a banquet was two cheeseburgers at McDonald's. His gift to the poor was born out of his suffering. For just three years earlier the newborn daughter placed in his arms looked strong and healthy in every way, but was later found to be mentally retarded. Loving church women welcomed her into the church nursery and later gave her special care as she moved up through the departments. In gratitude to these women, the father sought a way to thank God which could bring others with a hurt into God's building.

Since he was the maitre d'hotel of a large Cleveland club, it seemed natural to give his gift through food. Before long an "Arabian-night-like" series of dinners was being given to the poor of Cleveland. I joined other women in polishing our finest silver dishes and learned to make French sauces and to decorate gourmet platters.

At six o'clock, with ice molds in place and candles lit, the young father opened the door. For a moment the simply-dressed people filing in just stared, too shocked to speak. Could all this magnificence be for them for the thirty-five cents they held in their hands? But it was for them. They could tell by welcoming smiles. At first they hesitated to lift silver forks, to disturb the beautiful platters. But soon their plates were piled high and chatter filled the room.

More beautiful than the food was the young father's face as he watched their pleasure. His smile said simply, "We love you," just as his hands had done in the long hours of preparation.

Love freely given can open the hearts of God's battered people. If there is "room in the inn" for them, there may in turn be room in *their hearts* for God.

76

NINE Spilled Pitchers

The New Orleans tour bus jostled me against Hugh's shoulder while young Hugh stared out the window across from us. Our jocular driver paused to ask each of us where we had come from. When we said Minnesota, he chuckled a moment, then swung around in his seat. "That there is the Mississippi River," he said pointing. "It begins up in your state; Minneapolis takes a sip, turns back what it don't want; St. Louis takes some more, then dumps back its wastes. Twenty-five hundred miles and sixteen cities' effluent later, it arrives here in New Orleans —and there it is, our drinking water."

I had never before thought of the thousands of people who drink water drained out of my kitchen sink. We do have a responsibility for water purity for those who drink after us. And so it is with spiritual things. As God fills us, we are meant to be tipped up, that his living water may through us fill others. We had begun a pilgrimage, had found a meeting place with God. Now it was time to spill over lest his living water evaporate from disuse.

Meanwhile, what was God doing in our lives as a family? We were more honest with each other. We could discuss hurt pride without the alienation of anger. We were one in Christ, and that brought a continuing flow of love. But though united in Christ, we are each individuals in our relationship to God. And because this must be so, each of us flowers spiritually according to talents given to us alone and in direct ratio to our making ourselves available to God.

As our relationship with God differs, so do our direction and activity vary. Family faith is not attainable by family heredity or by Bible osmosis, though it is true that background has a great deal to do with nurturing God's seed. Rather, each of us becomes a whole person as he allows God to mold him.

So it was with our family: Hugh, Sr. in his business world; Gail, a mother and wife and artist; young Hugh, a student; and me, meant to be a hub of family life, but sometimes feeling more like a doormat. Where had we been; where were we going? Big questions call for big answers.

When Gail was about four, I often envied her uncomplicated relationship with God. Many days her record player droned constantly, but we rejoiced that out of our classical record collection more were played than stepped or sat upon. One particular morning Lohengrin's wedding music poured forth. I tiptoed up the stairs with an arm load of ironing, and paused to watch a scene in a deep bay window. A procession of over-dressed dolls marched around Gail's crossed legs. Morning sunlight glinted gold off Gail's long hair, reflected bride doll's tiara and picked up the gold in the buttercups dangling from the doll's crossed hands. But hush, Gail is praying, "Please, God, make 'bridey' a good mommy. Now God, you can marry them."

Her sequence was mixed, but God understood. I slipped downstairs. I hadn't been invited to the wedding, but God had.

By the next day, records were neatly stacked, dolls placed in rows, our home dusted and rubbed into unnatural order for expected guests. Gail was bubble-bathed after being pried loose from beloved shorts and tee shirts, then pressed into blue organdy and starched pinafore. As a final chore, I swept the front porch clear of crunchy Catalpa leaves. All was in readiness. Now I could relax.

Just at that moment Gail whirled around the corner of the house, her pinafore pulled taut over a bundle of leaves. Before I could stop her, she dumped the pile over my clean porch.

"What in the world are you doing?" I screamed. "I just this minute swept this porch clean."

She looked up at me, her blue eyes innocent of guile, "Oh, Mommy, you worry so much. God will take care of the leaves. You'll see."

And he did. A strong breeze sprang up. In one blast the porch was cleared. How simple is the faith of a little child. I secretly wished I had a private chunk of my own.

Two moves later, during Gail's adolescent years, an unfriendly clique did little for her relationship with the church of our choice. Instead, an Episcopalian minister invited Gail to join her friend Mary on picnic supper outings Sunday evenings on his boat on Lake Michigan. Jesus' words as he spoke at the Sea of Galilee became real to the young people tossed in Lake Michigan's breezes. It was no accident when Gail later joined the Episcopal church on Purdue's college campus. Her fiancé, Peter, up from choir boy to Purdue Glee Club soloist, often met her at the chapel near their college housing.

Following their marriage five years later, they headed for Pensacola where Pete was a navy pilot. Meanwhile, we moved to Saint Paul. They had little inkling of the revolutionary change in our lives until we descended on them, armed with Bibles, tracts, and a new righteousness that blew with a holy gale. Or so we thought. For them, it was a hurricane. Mother, dad, and brother had become three pietists ready to transform them.

It was months before we understood their reluctance to grasp all that we wanted to give them. One day as I brushed Hugh, Sr.'s favorite velveteen jacket, I smiled at the sleeves hunched and wrinkled as though still stretched over his arms. On the floor below lay his deerskin slippers, vintage 1960, soled and resoled, the toes comfortably hunched up and heels worn down. Would I want these beloved clothes made like new? No, they were dear because they bore a familiar shape of a loved one.

So it was with Gail. She loved us as she knew us: me, full of clucking and tucking-in ways; her dad, fun loving and ready to fish with her at the drop of a line; and young Hugh, loaded with wisecracks, but tender underneath. She didn't want the three apostles from Saint Paul; she wanted us as she knew us. We loosened our biblical thumbtacks and found the air freer.

There is a question often asked, especially in evangelical circles, that baffled me while it seemed routine to others. "Tell me, is John or Mary a Christian?" I found with some I could easily say, "Oh, yes, he is really filled with the Spirit." While of others, in all honesty, I could only say, "He is active in the church." Some who could rattle off the date, hour and minute of their acceptance of salvation indicated no glow or joy of the Spirit.

I was especially disturbed when asked about the Christian status of our daughter Gail, for I knew that the things of God were tremendously important to her. One day I stopped struggling with this point. From then on, when questioned as to whether she was a born-again Christian, I replied, "That is between God and Gail, not for me to judge." Christ's words, "Judge not, that you be not judged" (Matt. 7:1), reinforced my thinking.

However, Christ's command warning us not to judge our fellowmen is one of the most difficult for me to follow. For instance, how can I presume to object to anyone judging my daughter or myself, when, instinctively, I tend to make snap judgments myself, unfounded by broader facts? Wasn't I, in a sense, judging the Christianity of those I visited in the churches on our earlier church hunt, by the flimsy question, "What do you do for a living?" and by the untidy looks of a few? Again, at the drunken dinner party described early in this book, can the true worth of these people be judged in one scene? Certainly Noah would have been passed over on that basis except for God's loving forgiveness. Over and over I find I must beware of judging and concentrate on loving.

On a following visit, Gail told us of a thrilling weekend retreat she spent during which she heard the Rev. Peter Lawson, an Episcopalian priest, tell a story that moved her deeply.

This young priest visited a catatonic woman (with schizophrenic symptoms involving muscular rigidity) in a psychiatric institution in Indiana. Day after day it was as though he talked to a stone. Nothing about her moved, not even an eyelid, as he told her of Christ's love for her. In spite of this he continued his visits, determined to melt her with love. One day he received word that he was to move to another diocese. The next day he told the woman, "This is the last time I can visit with you for I am being transferred. I shall continue to pray for you and God will go on loving you."

To his amazement, a tear rolled down her cheek, her eyes blinked. Then, like a windup toy, her legs began to move. Like an image of wood she moved slowly toward a cabinet. Fumbling fingers opened the door, scraped something from the metal shelf. As one in a trance, she moved toward him, holding her hand grotesquely forward. Her hand unlocked. Inside, was a piece of gray bread. She divided it. Now tears coursed down her cheeks. The largest piece she thrust into the priest's mouth, the smaller into her own. Through cracked lips, she mumbled, "Communion."

As Gail finished telling me the priest's story, both of us blinked back tears. "I'll never forget that weekend, mother. This is what God means to me. His love in us can melt a heart turned to stone. That is what I want to do, love enough to help people."

Giving and loving are Gail's way of sharing Christ. On our last visit Gail and Pete drove in just as we did. They had put a young couple just recovered from a serious accident on a plane to join their children for Christmas with the ministering grandparents. Well, I thought, I can leave the spiritual judgments up to God. Giving and loving are certainly part of the fabric of God.

As for our son, Hugh, his life had really opened up. In those beginning days as a new Christian, he groaned when kids said, "Pardon me" when they found themselves swearing in front of him. At such times he felt like a kind of "pariah" (set apart more by virtue than sin) when he wanted just to be part of the gang. Before long he teamed up with two guys, one a talented actor and the other a brilliant son of a missionary. Together they developed music and humor that led to emceeing and radio shows. Like the "Peanuts" characters, Hugh found satire a good tool to use for Jesus Christ.

Another Day, Another Miracle

When in his junior year at Moundsview High School he was selected by his classmates as their representative to Minnesota Boys State, he was pleased. Already he had an interest in politics encouraged by his participation as president of his class and vice-president of the Student Council. He felt confident, that is, until he arrived at Gustavus Adolphus College.

It didn't take him long to discover that he was surrounded not only with brains, brawn, and ego, but by kids that had been coached by lawyer dads in political savvy to ensure being elected governor of Boys State. This was the world of hand-shaking, political promises and skilled maneuvers. Where did he fit in? He didn't. He felt like yesterday's leftover hamburger. He felt even worse when he learned the credentials of the other 450 delegates, any one of whom seemed more qualified than himself.

Going back over that day with his dad, he said, "I was used to running for office, but that kind of backslapping, handshaking, phoney bargaining for votes floored me. It wasn't real, just a hyper-ego trip, the opposite of Christianity. I couldn't play that game.

"I felt I had to get away, to talk to the Lord. Up in my room, I put it to him; 'Lord, you know I planned to run for governor, but not that way. As I see it, I don't have a chance of winning. If you want me to be governor, you'll have to put me in the right places and give me the right words to say. But then, maybe you just want me to make friends for you.' "

After prayer, Hugh felt better. From then on he was convinced that he was to use this opportunity to share his belief in Christ and to get to know the other guys as individuals. This he did. He ignored those handing out campaign buttons and brochures touting their gubernatorial qualifications. Instead he began sharing with other lonely kids in small groups his relationship with Christ with no intention of gathering support for his candidacy.

Meanwhile, the kids were becoming involved in city, county, and state elections as well as preparing for larger state contests in line with the planned Legion program.

To Hugh's amazement, he was nominated and elected municipal court judge by the fellows in his city group. Then, at the same time, he was selected to chair his precinct caucus at the County Convention.

For the first time Hugh heard his name mentioned as his party's nominee for governor. "I figured," he told us, "I was the only one who hadn't already alienated a lot of people with a premature campaign, but I couldn't believe the support I was getting from my delegation without any personal campaign.

"But at the same time I heard ugly muttering from supporters of another candidate within my own party. This wasn't what I wanted. How could I share Christ when I was the focus of ill will?

"I took this new problem to God. I paced my room all evening and prayed. I felt even less sure than I had that first lonely evening. I finally phoned Dad, told him my problem and asked him to come to the campus to pray with me. I'd always been able to count on him before and I sure needed him now. When he arrived I was still pacing and tearing my hair over the speech I had to prepare for the Convention the next day. I was no closer to knowing what to say.

"Late into the night Dad and I prayed together. One thing began to come clear. My speech would be anything but political. It would center around principles in politics, using the Christian life as an example of how to solve problems, both in our personal lives and in political situations. Dog-tired, we finally slept.

"A few hours later I faced my main opponent on the Convention floor. To my surprise, I received the county nomination on the first ballot. Now supported by my county for the State Convention, I continued to tell how Christ had changed my life and could make significant changes in other lives. I also told how politics can become corrupt and bitterly self-centered unless approached from the Christian viewpoint, that all that we do should be done for the good of others first, and that we must put political ambitions aside. I announced my slogan 'Principles, not politics.' "

Hugh witnessed all around him vote-trading and bargaining in which issues and people were not considered. His backers felt that by now he probably had enough votes, but he felt such trading and bargaining was the wrong approach. Hugh rose before the group and asked for the floor to make a motion. "I propose," he stated, "that no previous bargaining be recognized by any delegation and that voting be done on an individual basis rather than by delegates' blocs and *only* on the basis of quality of the candidates and their speeches." There was no discussion. The motion was unanimously passed by bloc votes and its success greeted by a standing ovation. Hugh felt this was at least in line with his slogan "Principles, not politics".

At the State Convention he was given the nomination of his Nationalist party as opposed to the Federalist and the campaign swung into full gear. Posters plastered the halls, leaflets were given out, campaign speeches followed one another by members of his party. At that time he laid down the rule that his name never be posted or printed except when accompanied by the total list of nominees for all positions.

Word filtered back that the Federalist candidate was an exceptionally fine speaker and had a commanding personality. Once again Hugh became apprehensive about his ability to represent his party. The climax of all the tension and uncertainty came when one of the legion counselors confronted Hugh. "I don't know how you got so far with a campaign like yours," he mumbled through a dangling cigar, "but I want you to know that it is offensive to some legionnaires. I think you should find something else to talk about in your final speech." He glared at Hugh, then strode off.

Hugh's relations with his advisory counselors had been excellent. This was completely unexpected. "I was really confused," he said. "I didn't know what to do. To water down my testimony seemed to deny all I had tried to do so far and I felt my only reason for having this opportunity was to tell about the Lord."

He was prepared personally to suffer the consequences of resigning, but was concerned about the boys who backed him and their right to win. Weighing it all carefully, he determined to go ahead and give his testimony even though he now felt he had no chance to win. Again he paced and prayed through another sleepless night.

Out of the night's agonizing, somehow he incorporated his testimony into a prepared speech delivered before the Boys State body the following evening. Ballots were cast, and he went to bed that night at least feeling that he had taken best advantage of the opportunity the Lord had given him, regardless of the outcome.

The next morning at breakfast the announcement rang out, "Hugh McLeod is the new governor of Boys State." God had accomplished the impossible. Hugh sat stunned while many hands reached out to him, hoisted him on the shoulders of his party members, carried him triumphantly in a roar of cheers. From a corner of the noisy hall, he noticed another legion counselor beckoning him. Managing to shake loose from his puzzled friends, he edged toward the counselor who quickly pulled him aside. He spoke with difficulty.

"I don't know what you and your counselor talked about, but last night he died of a coronary. His last words were, 'Tell Hugh McLeod I'm not against his religion. My concern is for Boys State.' "

The news of the counselor's death jolted the assembly, but no one was more rocked than Hugh. Hugh said, "To learn the last words the man said concerned me was something to think about."

Becoming governor gave Hugh a chance to speak of his faith over TV as well as to many gatherings throughout the state. "I learned," he said, "that God can use me only when I let him take over."

TEN **Why Do They Do These Things?**

It is scarcely necessary to travel abroad to discover new cultural experiences or to get to know people of other nations. Gold-threaded saris and Muslim turbans mingle with fringed jeans and yarn stoles on sprawling campuses. Not long ago I heard a student from Iraq, then in graduate studies at the University of Minnesota, say forcefully, "Why is it that you Christians spend huge sums to train and send missionaries overseas when you could make friends with students from abroad right on your own campus and tell them about Christ? It's the international student who should then carry the message back to his homeland.

"I heard of Christ in Iraq," he continued, "through my fellow countryman, returned from an American campus. While he lived among you, he found Christ's way and later told me. Naturally I preferred to listen to him than to a stranger who lived differently and spoke with a strange accent.

"Do you know," he continued, "there are hundreds of international students who stay four to seven years in your land and are never invited into an American home? Why aren't you missionaries to the stranger in your midst?"

A stranger in our midst and we refuse to take him in! How can we toll our church bells and ignore Jesus' commandment to "love our neighbor as ourselves"? I felt guilty every time I saw a sari in the supermarket.

Another Day, Another Miracle

It was autumn with flaming leaves when I finally called the Minnesota International Center of the University. A voice with a Chinese accent answered my offer of friendship. "Would you be able to meet a young scientist from India? He is due to arrive at the Saint Paul—Minneapolis airport on Friday? He will need help, for he is already one week late for classes."

I agreed, read the literature they mailed, and tackled the pronunciation of his name. At noon on Friday I faced the Northwest Airlines ramp, conspicuous with a sign across my chest reading, "Welcome Ramesh Patil!"

The crowd paid little attention. Then I saw him—a slightly stocky, fine-looking young man wearing a sport jacket and slacks. He hesitated, scanned the crowd, then smiled broadly as he read my sign. We introduced ourselves. His English was flawless and his manner courtly.

Later, he often referred to that moment saying, "Mrs. McLeod, from the moment I saw you there at the airport to greet me, I knew all would go well for me in this new land." Such a little gesture, but it was an omen to him. A student from the university assisted in registering and settling him. I learned that many students come to Minnesota with only sweaters and sandals to protect them in our severe weather. To meet their needs, clothing and furniture are stored in the International Center garage.

Patil, as we call him, is a brilliant and friendly person. Immediately he became a special addition to our family though he lived in a tiny apartment off campus. Since he was strictly vegetarian, I struggled with recipes recommended by the University; but, to us, they were tasteless. I soon discovered rice pilaf which has become our family favorite and which Patil declared "excellent" with his ceremonious bow and sweeping gesture.

Our friendship grew as we shared meals together, as well as Indian films at the University with him. We delighted in his high moral values, felt ashamed at times when forced to explain pornography and sexual license on the American scene. He accepted his new life with enthusiasm and worked doggedly in his graduate studies in geology.

Why Do They Do These Things?

He soon bought a secondhand car and mastered driving it in the way he tackled everything—as a scientific experiment to be performed with excellence. We knew there were times when he missed his attractive wife, Indira, teaching back in her home village, and his bright-eyed son, Shivaj. Their pictures dominated his small off-campus rooms.

No eight-hour shift suited Patil. He rose at dawn, ate a sack lunch at his office, and regularly worked on into late evening. In record time, he earned his master's degree and proceeded with his doctorate. Summers, he worked in the Duluth area studying rock formations—study which served as a foundation for later scholarly papers of world impact.

But what was God doing in our international friendship? For one thing, he caused me to study more about India, beginning with *The Discovery of India* by Jawaharlal Nehru[1] and a small book called *Christ of the Indian Road.*[2] In the latter book, to my sorrow, I read over and over statements by native Indians to this effect: "If I had met one professing Christian who truly lived like Christ, I would have followed your Christ." How terrible, with all our missionaries, they couldn't find one. Would Patil find one here in a nation often called Christian? His dark eyes always seemed to be searching after truth.

Patil was Hindu and I wasn't sure what that meant. I knew he acknowledged God, had studied in a Catholic school system. He often said, "With God's grace," and thanked God for the good happenings in his life.

One evening we took him to the Hilton Hotel for a Christian Business and Professional Couples Club banquet. We had previously watched his amazement as he counted rows of seats at an ice show at Saint Paul's Coliseum. Now we wondered how he would react to the chandeliers and brocade of the Hilton. But he said little of his surroundings, instead listened carefully to the speaker, a renowned young scientist who told of his former drug problems and finally of Christ's revitalization of his life. The scientist spoke well; time passed all too quickly.

Later, as we headed for the car ramp, Patil fairly bounced on his feet. "I think I finally understand something I have been wondering about you both, Mr. and Mrs. McLeod," he began.

Another Day, Another Miracle

"I knew there was something different about you, but I couldn't figure out what it was. Is it for you like the young scientist?" His dark eyes searched our faces in the dim light as we walked.

"Yes, Patil, this happened to us too," we agreed smiling.

"When?" he asked.

"About three years ago," Hugh replied.

"So that is it. I knew there was something special, but what it was and when it happened puzzled me. Please have the kindness to tell me about it," he pleaded. Though Patil was of small stature in this Scandinavian area, his intensity made him a powerful force.

What a time to be in a darkened car without access to our helpful booklet by Campus Crusade called *The Four Spiritual Laws*. But perhaps it was as well. Patil wanted no "canned' presentation. He simply wanted our story of how we received Christ. As the words tumbled out, he listened attentively.

"So that is it," he said, letting the wonder of it all settle into the silence.

"Would you like this experience, Patil?" I asked, trying to hold in my eagerness. I handed him a booklet about the scientist we had just heard that told how to obtain such an experience.

"I shall read your little booklet and think about it. It has been a splendid evening and I'm happy to know about your experience."

The next time we met, Patil spoke warmly of the booklet and announced, "With God's grace, I'm making arrangements to bring Indira and Shivaj here. All is being put in order for their passports and to secure a larger apartment."

We delighted in the news. It had been a long lonely time for all of them. Meanwhile, an exquisite golden sari arrived in the mail, a gift from Indira, who promised to show me how to wear it.

She was even lovelier in person than her picture promised, with a natural grace and dark curls around her face. Their son, Shivaj, raven-haired like his parents, was a delightful, energetic boy. We learned that Shivaj had become ill on the flight, needing the attention of a doctor on arrival in New York. He recovered quickly, but not his mother. She was tense with worry over his health and doubted the wisdom of leaving India. After all, first there had been difficulty in obtaining passports and then Shivaj's illness. Had God wanted her to stay at home, she wondered.

She visited our home for the first time on Thanksgiving day. So much was different in America. They looked wonderingly at our turkey, then passed it by, filling their plates from trays of fruit and vegetables. In addition our uncovered legs must have shocked them, for I later learned that a respectable lady in Madras is careful that her sari just touch the floor.

A few weeks later, Indira asked me to wear the golden sari to a college Christmas concert. I hesitated at first, feeling it inappropriate for me, but finally agreed. I'm glad I did, for it helped me realize how lonely it can be to attend a large gathering and be dressed differently.

Patil's joy was evident as he relaxed his long working hours a bit to enjoy his family. Shivaj delighted in exploring American mechanical wonders, but Indira found both the cultural shock and her religious qualms too much for her gentle spirit. She soon became seriously ill. Just prior to Christmas, she was placed in University Hospital. We rushed over one snowy afternoon. It was a shock to see her weakness and pallor. Patil, always the gracious host, placed chairs beside her bed.

"I'm so happy to see you," she cried, leaning forward. "Something amazing happened to us. But Patil will tell it."

"Yes, I want to tell you about it," he began slowly, clearing his throat. "Yesterday as I was leaving the hospital, I had almost reached the elevator. A young Chinese man approached me, obviously in a hurry. He stopped suddenly and asked, 'Pardon me for stopping you, but I am searching for someone. . . . It may sound odd, but I had left the hospital when I had the strongest feeling someone needed spiritual help. You see, I'm a chaplain, a former Buddhist turned Christian. Could you know anyone with such a need?' "

"For a moment, I just stared at him," Patil said. "How could he know how troubled Indira and I felt with her illness and homesickness? 'I wonder if it could have been us. We really need help,' I told him."

Another Day, Another Miracle

"Indira was surprised to see me return with the young chaplain. After introducing him, I quickly explained our meeting. He prayed a beautiful prayer with us and was most kind. Then we showed him the little booklet you gave me some time ago."

It was our turn to be surprised. They had kept the booklet all this time and even taken it to the hospital. It must mean something to them.

But the medical news was not good. The doctors were unable to understand why diet and drugs didn't improve Indira's health. Her eyes were dark with fear lest she die in this strange land. She begged to leave at once for India, but was too ill to even leave the hospital. As for her husband, he was torn between his desire to keep his family with him and his concern for her health.

He had still another problem, that of transportation to the hospital, for his car refused to start. The night before we left for a Christmas visit to our daughter, we brought our second car, a sturdy Buick, over to his apartment so that he might use it while we were gone. His worry about his wife showed in his hollow eyes and his clothes, suddenly too roomy. He served us nuts and chilled juice, chatting graciously, but we knew he was wrestling with the decision of what was best for his family.

After we finished eating, he seated himself by us, leaned forward and asked, "There is something I am unable to understand." He bit his lip, continued, "You have come to us with gifts of food, the decorations, but now most of all, the car. Do you know what a car like that means in my country? Only very important persons would have such a car, and they would treat it with extreme care. And what do you do? You bring it to me so that I may visit my wife in the hospital. It will have to stand out in the snow instead of in your garage, you know."

"It's used to snow," I interrupted, smiling.

"How can you trust me with your lovely car? I was telling my friend from India about all this. Do you know what he said to me? 'Patil, tell me why do they do these things?' But I couldn't answer him. Now I will ask you. . . . Why do you do these things?"

I started to smile again, but there was no looking away

from the question in his eyes. He was deeply serious. "Why, I suppose it just seems natural when God gives you much, to want to share it. Besides, we wouldn't be using the car while we visit Gail. That is no great sacrifice on our part."

But it went deeper with him than that. For the question still hung there. I had to think, Why *do* we really do it? I was embarrassed to say it. It came out in a whisper, "It's what Christ would want us to do."

"Ah," he said, still thinking. Would he understand what I meant? Such a little thing to do, but it wasn't small to him, and that's what counted. Sometimes ordinary gestures mean more than extravagant gifts in friendship.

January was a grim month. Indira recovered enough to return to India with Shivaj. Left behind, Patil locked up his heart and plunged day and night into his graduate studies. He began avoiding friends for inevitably they asked the question, "Why did your wife return to India?" It did no good to reply, "To regain her health." For most went on to tell him of all they knew who endured loneliness to stay on in America.

We missed him, worried about his monastic life. Though we met at intervals, we knew it was a strain for Patil to come out. The sooner he completed his doctorate, the sooner he could return to his family in India. We admired and loved him but could do little but pray for him in his loneliness. Just before his return to India at the completion of his doctorate, we ourselves moved from Saint Paul. When God admonished us to "love thy neighbour as thyself" (Lev. 19:18), how truly he spoke. For a part of us is in India with Patil and his family. We miss them especially at Thanksgivings for their places at our table are empty.

Somehow I suspect that the same loving God loves us all, and I am content that each should find his own approach to God's doorsteps. Patil, in his gracious way, listened to us. We owe him the same privilege in his relationship to his God.

Ideally, caring and sharing Christ go hand in hand. But, unfortunately, the neighbors of some Christians may get the impression that the whole point of being neighborly is to cram the gospel down their throats.

Another Day, Another Miracle

The Good Samaritan story is an example of a person caring for a human being in distress. However, no mention is made of the Samaritan either evangelizing or witnessing to the victim of robbery. One thing alone motivated the Good Samaritan. His heart was moved by compassion. God creates openings when we may share Christ's way with others. Love is the best communicator. Without love it is easy to blunder and *even repel others*.

We know, for we made the mistake of over-urging a couple to attend a church function. Because we had been friends for some time, we knew of the man's aversion to churchy doings, an aversion resulting from a boyhood experience. But we also knew of his wife's longing for the things of God. We made an issue of their attending an international dinner at our church which nearly rocked our friendship. We learned from this sad experience that nothing good is accomplished by attempting to propel friends against their wishes into church-related activities.

Another possible hazard in evangelizing may be the attitude, "How many souls have you saved?" The first time I heard that phrase, I recoiled. All I could think of was Indians counting scalp locks on a pole. Fortunately, our missionary from Ethiopia sat next to me as this particular question was raised.

"Do you believe *we* save souls, Thelma?" I asked her.

"No, Ceil," she replied. "It is Christ who saves souls. I believe that we only help bring others to a point where they can personally receive him. Often there are many who play a part in bringing one person to what we Christians call the 'throne of grace.' "

I nodded, relieved. How many had it taken to bring me to the point of being reborn in Christ? First, I had to become a seeker to even start the journey. Then there were the girls with the joyous faces and worn Bibles who listened to my questions, the strangers in the hospital who gave me Communion, Catherine Marshall's book that became for a time my church experience, friends at Christian Women's Club and at Bible study, and finally, Pastor Frykholm who asked the question, "Is there anyone here for whom I may pray?"

Why Do They Do These Things?

My thoughts were interrupted as chairs scraped behind me. Thelma slipped into her pink coat. "You know, Thelma, I was thinking of all who helped me draw close to God," I said. "Perhaps we are really meant to be sort of way stations for our neighbors as they journey toward God. We may supply their physical needs or just one part of their spiritual need. It is God who puts the pieces all together until that soul is finally united with him."

Thelma's bubbly laugh rang out. "Yes, that's the way I like to think of it, Ceil. Each of our Ethiopian women comes to God in her own way. I'm just glad I can help a bit, maybe through aiding their understanding of the Bible, through prayer, or perhaps just by helping in their home."

On the way home the car radio gave a bulletin on Indonesia. I thought of the amazing happenings in that country from the time the political regime turned over with its resultant bloodbath to a climate where Christianity could grow openly. Under the former government, Christians had suffered terrible persecution, but were the first to protest the massacre of those who had injured them. Over and over those newly in power asked the Christians, "Why do you try to help those who hurt you?"

"Because *they* are our neighbors," they replied, "and Christ told us to love our neighbors as ourselves." Such love was beyond comprehension. Because of it, Christianity is making great strides today in Indonesia. There, the Bible is used as a teaching tool in the public schools, while in America it lies dusty on the library shelf.

Bangladesh is still another battered country, first ripped apart by hurricane, then by political and martial bloodbath. Now it too seems open as never before to the gospel. So often a nation that mends its wounds looks toward a loving God, and in turn finds his Son, Christ, who suffered long ago for each battered one among us.

We can be thankful that wounded nations like Indonesia and Bangladesh are drawing closer to God, we can pray that young men and women in India will reflect a true image of Christ, but we alone are responsible for strangers in our midst.

Will young men from Iraq, or Hong Kong, or Nigeria continue to learn about Christ on the American campus or in a neighboring home? Patil is back in India, but his compatriots are here, ready to ask, "Why do they do these things?" What answer will we give them?

ELEVEN Polly's Living Room, Dr. Wirt's Mountaintop, Rich's Church Pew

Where do miracles happen? If you were seeking, where would you expect to find them? Logically, in a church, a seminary, or at a religious meeting. And so you might, but the whole world is the backdrop against which we can see God's miracles performed. Therefore, you may meet God wherever you are—at the mailbox, on a mountaintop, at a country club.

Just how do we recognize these miracles of God? The first step is to prepare ourselves. I find that in a place apart from noise and crowds, I can put my spirit in readiness through prayer.

It was prayer that prepared the way for an encounter at a modern-structured church in Moorhead, Minnesota. Yes, we moved again, this time from Saint Paul to Moorhead. Sometimes I think these pages sound more like a travelogue with Gray Van Lines than an adventure story with God. There have been times when I felt that my husband's company must have a huge checkerboard with families plunked down as playing pieces to be moved about as though they were truly circles of painted wood.

At any rate, wearied with selling homes, we moved this time into a townhouse. Just a block away stood a large church with a roof shaped like a ski slope. Though we had already begun to attend another church, this slant-roofed church down the block concerned me. After all, for many years, earlier, we had been members of that particular denomination. In all that time we couldn't recall ever being asked to receive Christ. Perhaps there were some here, I pondered, who, like us, had somehow missed this invitation. I began to pray that God would give me a way to tell his story there. I had no idea how, but I trusted God to find a way.

And he did, but by way of a sort of detour. A month after our move, I was shut in with a recurrence of my spinal problem. Before this I had been chafing at my Christian inactivity, complaining to God at not being used in the old ways. Prayers and letters from friends plus the kindness of church acquaintances gave me not only joy, but a sense of peace. Most of all, I felt close to God. I came to learn this was God's way of preparing me for further usefulness to him. Now I could better understand Paul's restiveness as he waited at Tarsus, eager to be again on his missionary journeys.

Then the call came, not, as expected, from a hospital volunteer, Christian Women's Club, or a nursing home; but to speak at Triumph Church in early spring. A call to speak! I had done plenty of talking at PTA, hospital, and church meetings, but never as the formal program speaker on an inspirational program. I was terrified. God gave the gift of public speaking to both my husband and son, but I needed my thoughts written on notes or I became tongue-tied. Even phoning is something I avoid until the last moment. I prefer to send a note or write an article. But when you ask to be used and God paves the way, you dive in whether or not you can swim. So I dived. God has promised he'll not desert us, and he doesn't. That spring day my throat seemed to be one big nonswallow, my hands too frozen to turn my notes. I prayed desperately while I hunted for my handkerchief.

There it was. "Mrs. McLeod will now speak to us on 'Spring-time of the Heart.'" How could a frozen vegetable like me speak about thawing hearts, I wondered, as I pushed back my chair. I couldn't remember walking to the podium, but there I was and suddenly it was as though God scooped me up and said, "Look around, my daughter, they're women like you with needs just like yours. Tell them what I've taught you." The faces before me became not a hushed waiting audience, but women, trusting, listening, lovely vessels of God, and it was easy to talk to them.

Unknown to me at the time, a women's circle chairman from the slant-roofed church was an invited guest to Triumph that night. She approached me after the program saying, "I wonder if you would come and speak to our women's group. What you said about prayer healing and personal commitment to Christ would be meaningful to our ladies. Sometimes, I think we don't hear enough about knowing God personally."

I was almost too surprised to answer. Not only was I being asked to speak again, but to my prayer-concern church. Could this be God's answer? Why not? I have prayed to be used there. How marvelously God works out plans for us if we ask to be used for him.

The day I spoke at this church, a young woman with beautiful dark eyes listened intently. I learned later that she hadn't planned to attend that day. She needed time to work on her notes for the speeches she was called on to give at Christian Women's Clubs, churches, and Alcoholics Anonymous. But all morning she had felt an inner urge to go to her circle meeting. Finally just as the meeting opened, she slipped into a seat.

"Many of you have talents of which you know nothing now," I stated. At these words the young woman, Polly, leaned forward until I felt myself speaking to her directly. "God gave you these talents, but Christ can release them for his purposes. I never dreamed of being a writer," I continued, "until I wanted to tell the whole world about this new life I found in Christ. God sent me to a *Decision* School of Writing, surrounded me with writers who suggested tools, and now he has given me talented friends here with whom to begin a Christian Writers' Guild."

Later, Polly told me that she shivered when she heard those words. For she knew then why God urged her to attend. He wanted her to write her book and had used my talk to open the way for her to have help with it. Not long ago, Polly was an alcoholic herself, fearful of being alone, but trapped in her desperate habit. She wrestled with God as she wrestled with her thirst. The day she learned she was to become a grandmother, something within her broke. She wanted to be a whole person to this little new one. Somehow she must get control over herself. Christ gave her that control and also a radiant new self, a self that can in turn restore others.

With this new mission to tell others of Christ's way, Polly had to sort out invitations to speak. Meanwhile, she was unable to fill all requests. Maybe she could write her story so many more could read it than could hear her tell it. Her friends reinforced her desire, but how do you write a book? You need know-how, tools that were unkown to Polly, just as they had been to me.

Just as God sent Catharine and others to teach me how to write, he used me as a link to help Polly find her tools. This is the way he works.

Just as he planned the bridge rendezvous for me, he plans encounter points for others. Those who study the zodiac for signs, who dabble in witchcraft, who deal in world intrigue, are missing the real excitement and the true purpose of all time. They're playing for daily stakes and missing eternal treasure. If enough of us were truly "turned-on for Christ," how dramatic would be the meeting places. We would no longer need soap operas and an incessant diet of TV adventure stories, since no make-believe story can compare with God's adventures.

Several times earlier I have mentioned Christian Women's Club. This is no ordinary organization, but an international one without a membership list. Does that sound odd? It is, but it works. A few Christian women get together, arrange a meeting place for lunch or dinner, often at a country club, hotel, or restaurant. They seek out guest musicians plus a feature like a style show or a flower arrangement demonstration. Most important, however, is the speaker, usually a layman, who tells simply of dynamic changes in his or her life since it was turned over to Jesus Christ. No one is asked to be a member of Christian Women's Clubs, just invited to come to meetings as they choose. They have no dues, just take a collection to supply the needs of simple churches often set up in missionary homes in small villages where no church exists.

Instead of membership in a club, it is hoped that guests will become members of God's family, whatever their background, whether Protestant, Catholic, Jewish, or nonreligious. I mention these clubs because they provide a doorstep for many who may be "turned off" by or unacquainted with a local church. They provide a place to come and hear how others have received Christ.

Betty Denny was one who came to Christian Women's Club at Midland Hills Country Club, but she had no idea on that first visit of the drastic changes ahead of her. She'd been active in her church all her life, but she discovered this to be different from most of her usual church luncheons. As a decorator blended fabrics and wallpaper on a display board, she settled comfortably back in her chair. Everyone seemed friendly. The centerpiece flowers were special, made of some stiff red and white and blue fabric. The violinist was a concert artist. All this, she marveled, for the simple price of a luncheon!

Soon the speaker, Dr. Sherwood Wirt, editor of *Decision* magazine, was being introduced. "Some years ago," he began, "I was minister of a Presbyterian church in California. I was concerned: our attendance was down, and little wonder, for nothing much seemed to be happening in that congregation. How could I make God real to them unless I felt close to him myself? I knew I needed to get away where I could be alone with God. I spent days alone on a nearby mountain, reading the Bible and praying to be filled so that I might fill others. Gradually a kind of peace came over me, and certain Bible passages became meaningful. Not only did I feel changed, but on my return, the people listened in a new way; some who had stopped coming came back. I knew then that God was working in me."

Betty listened to Dr. Wirt as though he were talking directly to her. She had been wondering why her church life seemed monotonous sometimes, no matter how hard she worked at it. She began to wonder how she could renew her faith as had Dr. Wirt.

I met Betty as we served together on Christian Women's Board. After our business was concluded, we separated into groups of three or four to pray aloud together. Betty told me that this was the first time she had prayed aloud in a small group. It was new to me also and deeply meaningful. Both of us felt a deep love for our group. For Betty it was preparation for the days of suffering ahead. She was to find truth in God's promise that he will not send us trouble beyond our endurance.

On January 27, Betty and her husband Rich received a telegram from Vietnam sent by their son Dick's commanding officer. It read, "Your son Dick is seriously wounded with multiple shrapnel to the body and gunshot wounds in the face. Cause for grave concern."

Rich and Betty prayed together, then called the chairman of Christian Women's Club to ask for prayer. Next, Betty sent a wire to Dick, lying in a Vietnamese hospital, "The Spirit of the Lord is around you. Prayers of your friends encircle you. We are with you. There is no distance now. Christ makes all things near. You are not alone." Then just two days later Betty heard over the phone from Dick's wife these terrible words, "Dick is dead. He was in shock from the time his buddy found him."

From that day on Betty watched helplessly as her husband, Rich, moved around like a shadow that blotted out all around him. An airmail letter arrived with Dick's familiar handwriting on the outside, his last letter. Rich tore it open. A picture of a clean, smiling boy holding a machete fell out. Rich took the picture into his bedroom where he sat hour after hour staring at his son's face, his own face terrible, withdrawn.

Meanwhile, people streamed in and out of their home. Unable to take it any longer, Rich, bolstered and unsteady with tranquilizers, escaped to his office. Shortly after he left home Betty was called to the phone. "Your husband has collapsed," she heard. She rushed to him, took him to Abbott Hospital where he was placed in intensive care.

"We can't promise that he'll live, Mrs. Denny," the doctor said as he reached out to steady Betty. "He's in deep shock."

Betty pressed her lips together to keep from screaming. "Oh, God, not Rich too! I can't bear it. He's always been the strong one in our family."

Somehow she kept close to Rich, something kept her going hour after hour. Then he seemed compelled to talk. "You're lucky," he groaned, turning his head restlessly on his pillow.

"You have your friends at Christian Women's Club to pray for you. But I don't have even that though I've tried to be a Christian."

As Betty watched his anguish, she thanked God for her new ability to talk with him in prayer. A few days later, Rich, though still heavily despondent, insisted on coming home. The doctors advised Betty to keep him in the hospital at least two weeks, until after the funeral details were over. But Rich continued to insist on returning home. Already exhausted and torn with indecision over Rich's demands and his doctor's warnings, Betty slumped into her car, drove, scarcely noting where the wheels turned. Tears blurred her vision while weariness made each breath an effort. She slowed for young people at an intersection. One looked like Dick from the back. Oh, God, why couldn't he be here going to class again as these college students were doing? Two boys sat on the steps before a graceful stone building with "Saint Paul Bible College" cut in rough letters over the door. On impulse, Betty parked the car, walked toward the sitting boys. She had to tell someone. Maybe these kids would listen.

"May I talk to you?" she begged. They looked startled, but kind. The words tumbled out, first her son's death, now her husband near death, and the need for her to make a decision. As she talked a tear rolled down the cheek of one of the boys. The other put his arm around her just as Dick would have done. How good it felt!

"Let's go into the chapel and pray," the tall one said. "This is too much for you to decide alone. That's what God is all about." Such simple little prayers, almost whispers in the big room, but God listened and Betty felt comforted.

In the quiet, Betty made her decision. "I'm going to bring Rich home. He's only tearing himself apart there. I know he'd never forgive me if we didn't share these times together. Thank you, boys. I just know this is right. I'm sure God sent you to me today. I'll never forget it."

The next day Betty brought Rich home. His weakness terrified her, but it was still good to be together. Sunday followed. Could they—should they—go to church? Could Rich stand the commotion and the questions? She could see he dreaded going, but both felt they had to go.

Arriving late, they moved quietly into a back pew. As Betty looked at her husband's slumped shoulders, at beads of perspiration on his forehead, she wondered for the hundredth time if she had been wrong. She shuddered. Will he leave here on a stretcher, and will it be my fault?

Rich shifted his feet, reached for an orange bulletin in the pew before him. How can he read, Betty wondered, with his hand shaking so violently? To her amazement, he quieted, sat up straighter, staring intently at the orange paper. Betty leaned over to see what he was reading. His finger pointed to the words, "So that in one way or another I may save some, was Paul's goal."

With a swift movement, he grasped a pencil in the pew, crossed out the word Paul, wrote in, *Dick's Goal.* Then, he faced Betty, his eyes wider and bluer than she had ever seen them, "He just saved me," he whispered. "Someone just lifted a big load off my back that's been there since the telegram." Could this be the same man? she wondered.

Betty caught the fluttering paper as Rich started down the center aisle toward the altar for Communion, no longer shuffling in despair, now striding proudly. She hurried after him, tears of relief and joy trickling down her nose. "Oh, Dick, the same faith you had is now your dad's," she murmured soundlessly at the altar rail. "By faith, he, too, has received Jesus Christ as his Savior. God has comforted him and he's all right now. Thank you, God."

The words from a letter Dick sent to a Gold Star mother who had lost her son in battle awhile back flashed into her mind. "I'm not a hero, but I have a job to do. At the end of the year I pray that I will be alive and able to say, 'I've done my best.' Nevertheless, I pray that his will be done, for I know that it will be right, whatever may happen."

"Yes, Dick, God's will was done. You are with him, and because of your faith, your father has found peace with God. Bless you, and some day we'll all be together again." Betty took Rich's hand. Now they could be strong together.

I heard Betty tell this story a week after her husband's renewal in God. The ordeal showed in her hollow eyes, but from her agony a new power was born. She not only learned to pray for her need, but to pray for the needs of others.

In the days that followed, Betty took on herself the task of writing to mothers and wives throughout the state who had lost sons and husbands in Vietnam. Through her new faith, she comforted them. National recognition from President Nixon came to the Denny family, but they had little time for accepting applause. As for Rich, owner of a flourishing business, he found he could no longer use former methods of conducting business. More and more, Christ's demands drew him away from his own business. Finally, together, they asked God to help them decide what course Rich should pursue—the family business or a new unknown ministry. Though still uncertain of God's direction, they sold the business, content to wait on new orders. Meanwhile, Betty began to travel the state to speak at churches and Christian Women's Clubs. God was already using her to change lives for him.

Before long, Rich became director of Lutheran Youth Encounter at the University of Minnesota campus. Not only had he changed within, but there is now a vital dynamism about him that is contagious. The grim face of the despondent father I first met is scarcely recognizable in the youthful man with sparkling eyes who spoke to our church adult class just one year later. The heritage of new life he had received through faith following the death of a beloved son was evident.

From the Dennys I came to understand Saint Francis of Assisi's words, "It is in dying that we are born to eternal life." For it is not enough to be penetrated once for God. The dynamic Christian will have a series of encounters as he continues to surrender himself to the Lord of his life. Our growth occurs, I found, as we continually submit chunks of ourselves to God.

But each of us must have a meeting place. Polly found her miracle on her knees in her living room, Dr. Wirt found his on a mountain, Betty in a college chapel while God readied her for his service to other heartbroken mothers. Rich found God in a church pew with a piece of orange paper in his hand.

Another Day, Another Miracle

Have you experienced the miracle of the presence of God? Are you prepared to weather trouble when it strikes? Your miraculous encounter with God may be only minutes away.

TWELVE **Adopted into a Royal Family**

An adventure with Christ depends first on being a *willing* adventurer, then on finding a meeting place with God, next on growth in knowledge, and on dependence on him. So fortified, the dynamic *journey* begins—that of helping to transform other lives through Christ.

The first two steps, seeking and receiving Christ, can be taken by a person alone with God, but the next—the growing—often needs the loving help of another.

An infant at birth goes about the business of *becoming* someone, but equally important is his need of *belonging* to someone. Even though his nursery contains the latest equipment, if his need for belonging is not met, he can never develop normally. Like the infant, each of us has a tiny pocket of loneliness which may at times overwhelm us, depending on our relationship with others.

From earth's beginning God knew we needed a family. Why else did he send his son into a family situation? In addition, he elected to be our loving father. Of no less importance were his guidelines for living according to his commandments. But, unlike some earthly fathers, God never denies his love and forgiveness, no matter how far we turn from his ways.

As long as I can remember, I had prayed, "Our Father who art in heaven," but until my new life in him, I never thought of myself as his daughter; a servant, yes; a follower, yes; but a true daughter—incredible!

However, we learn of Jesus that, "as many as received him, to them gave he power to become the sons [daughters] of God" (John 1:12). It is a fact. I am a daughter of God! Since Christ is a king, I am a member of a royal family. In addition, I have many royal brothers and sisters both on earth and in heaven.

Just as we Christians are never again really alone or unloved when we become adopted into God's royal family, from then on we also belong to others in a special new way. Their needs are ours and we care about them even though our backgrounds may be culturally miles apart. We have prayer support that non-Christians may not have; we are linked by Bible truths in a world that has lost its standard of worth. Our royal family link becomes more important than genealogical ties.

But to return to the journey—any journey involves preparation, packing, touring, meeting emergencies enroute, and a return to home base. The Christian adventure is no different. First a person becomes aware of the need for a change; he next investigates the cost (in this case whatever will right him in his estrangement from God). His packing stage would involve becoming a seeker. Meeting Christ starts the tour, which in turn catapults the traveler into situations which call for adapting to new ways that God sets. Home for the Christian is heaven, for the journey once begun, never ends.

Anyone who has taken a package tour soon discovers bonus side trips enroute, frequently at extra expense, but often too exciting to pass up. On a recent European tour, we rushed through Holland, Germany, Austria, and parts of Italy in four days, reaching Rome with two free days to spend at will. Part of our tour group elected a side trip to Capri. However, we used our time to rinse out accumulated laundry, wander leisurely through the Borghesa Museum, plus shopping and eating at tucked-away restaurants. Later when we heard glowing reports of the beauty of Capri, we questioned our choice of routine sightseeing and leisure.

Similarly, it is easy for the new Christian to settle into routine church activity with its abundant busyness and miss the breathtaking sight of changed lives. Not that lives are not changed within the church. But, ideally, God's church should be a harbor that provides comfort, Bible education, and worship, but is ultimately a place from which to embark.

The Christian adventure is often called a journey inward and a journey outward. The journey outward involves telling others what it is like to know God—a sort of "show and tell." I state "show" first, because unless love is demonstrated, who will listen to Christ's story?

However, some new Christians, like sponges, receive Christ, become soggy with spiritual water, but are unable to squeeze themselves out for others. Elena was such a one. She grew up in a small town in a loveless home. Even worse, she was told that her parents married only because her birth was imminent. They used her to deflect their hate-filled barbs, until she grew to believe she was the cause of their unhappiness. Added to this was an early experience that she found too degrading to describe to anyone for years. All this boiled inside the girl, making her emotionally insecure and therefore unable to cope with school, though mentally able.

At fifteen, as a church visitor, Elena discovered a new relationship with Christ. It was a turning point in her life. Her family attended her baptism, but seemed unable to understand the change in their daughter. Inexorably, as Elena found her family reacting against her new ways, her inner glow began to fade.

Just as God cares about our finding a place where we can feel comfortable and loved, so also he knows that each of us needs someone who cares about us personally.

Elena had neither such a place nor loving relationship. How could she comprehend the warmth of God's love when she knew no human love?

A few years after her baptism experience I met her and learned of her many needs. While she was already getting psychological help for her emotional problems, I determined to be her friend no matter what difficulties presented themselves. In her gratitude, she bought us extravagant gifts, bicycled out six miles with a birthday cake balanced on shaky handlebars, painted our picket fence without complaining about a toe broken in an abrupt stop on her way to our home. She literally wrapped herself around us. We were the teddy bear, the rocking chair, the story time she had never had. In an adolescent, this can be hard to take.

How often we gave her back to God and asked for a breather. Meanwhile, she listened, not just to an overabundance of advice, but to the language of a loving family—how they laughed together, how they looked at each other. Fortunately, we didn't realize at the time that we were on stage. We made many mistakes and were far from ideal, but unless we are human how can another learn from us?

At any rate, months and years passed as Elena grew inside to fit her physical maturity. Meanwhile others reached out to her, giving her another side of love. At times she imitated her friends, becoming a sort of ersatz person. Invariably depression followed. I encouraged her to reach out to others with their problems, believing this would help her, but her own were too great. All she could do was to spill over with her troubles, which tended to drive away new friends.

One day I read an article by Dr. Paul Tournier, renowned Swiss psychiatrist, in which he stated that persons who have been dominated by other people need a milieu, a circle, a community; that is, a place in which to become a person. In other words, such people need to receive before they can give, since no one can give what he does not have.[1]

Elena first had to find her real self before she could, like the sponge, give water to others who were thirsty. It took months of loneliness, rebellion, study, and love before she had the courage to find out exactly who she was in God's eyes. Today she is a new radiant self, married to a fine young man. They know their income will be small and their problems huge, but they also know they are children of God and a trinity of love with their heavenly Father.

It took years for Elena to come to know the language of love. It was equally difficult for us to reestablish a comfortable relationship with Hugh's mother when it was jarred loose by our new life in Christ. Like so many new Christians enthralled with their mystic glow, we poured out our joy to Hugh's mother, wanting her to don the new bonnet of Christ immediately.

Hugh's mother, an attractive widow, visited us regularly. A highlight of her day was the five o'clock cocktail hour, usually just a glass of sherry, never much more, but a time to relax and chatter together. Simultaneously with the advent of our new life, the cocktail or two before dinner had slipped unnoticed out of our day. But what we didn't realize was that our new life had done nothing about Hugh's mother's old life. In our selfishness, we ignored her sherry time and simply upped our dinner hour. Looking back, we realize we could easily have shared a coke or a cup of coffee with her so that five o'clock was still a bright interlude in her long day. Then again, we were always rushing off to some religious meeting. We thought only of our disappointment in her not joining us, rather than of her disappointment in our leaving her so often.

Toward the end of a visit, she said words that haunted us both: "Hugh, I liked you better before you became a Christian!"

This really hurt for she was a special mother and dearly loved. On her next visit, she was to have a checkup at Mayo Clinic which might lead to serious surgery. I canceled out my calendar, prepared food for my family, and packed for a week with her at Rochester. Just before leaving on Sunday, Pastor Frykholm, whom she really liked, skipped dinner to see her.

As he removed his rubbers, I called down the stairs, "Here it is a half hour after church, and we know you have a meeting shortly. You won't even have time for a peanut butter sandwich today. That's hardly a day of rest for you."

His deep laugh rang out as he seated himself next to Hugh's mother. "What does that matter? Sunday is the Lord's day and how better can I spend it than here with your mother?"

She loved his answer. It was obvious he cared about her. In the future his words often returned to me. Whatever the task, I find if I begin with "This is the Lord's morning, how shall I spend it?" the day becomes exciting.

But back to mother. During the week we spent at Rochester, I was able to be with her constantly without interruption of children, phone, or schedule. She knew my whole concern was for her and her health and well-being. I no longer pushed spiritual matters, just loved her. That marked the end of her feeling alienated because of my new relationship with Christ. Her journey was her own, my gift to her the freer love I had because of Christ.

Not only was I now a daughter of God, but I was also a daughter to my husband's mother. My love needed to bridge our differing ways, not push her out of our relationship.

True love involves listening to the problems of another like Elena. It also involves loving another without trying to change that one, being content to let that one seek God's direction for himself. Love also is concerned with giving of itself in a flowing as delicate as the tiny tributaries of a great river.

Such love had come to me one March when our son was a third-grader. Bare branches screeched against my bedroom window as young Hugh laid a tray across my knees. His eyes blinked an apology for milk slopped from the cereal bowl to the limp paper napkin beneath. "Will you really be all right, Mom?" he asked.

"Yes dear, thanks for everything. I'll be fine. Hurry or you'll miss your bus."

"OK," he mumbled, already tripping downstairs.

But was I fine? Chills and pain on moving denied it. And what a time to be ill with my husband at an honors convention in Georgia for four days. He'd worked too hard for this for me to call him home.

As I spooned soggy cereal, I gulped down a pill delivered by the local pharmacy to stall off my old, familiar kidney infection.

As morning dragged on, I scrunched around in my lumpy bed, longing for just one good library book as I reread last month's *Reader's Digest*.

The back door scraped open. "Yoo-hoo," my next door neighbor Marian's voice called. "Can I come up?"

"Please do," I answered. How does she know? I wondered.

Her arthritic hands clutched a tray over which a cloth of dainty embroidered violets hung. A bright-jacketed book was tucked under one arm. "I saw young Hugh at the bus stop this morning," she said between breaths. "Thought you might like a sandwich." Though her voice was casual, her kind eyes inventoried my needs.

"How like you, Marian," I said gratefully. "What a pretty napkin this is."

"Knowing how you love wild flowers, I decided to use this. It won't be long before the real ones bloom, will it?"

While she described the heating of a casserole already tucked into the refrigerator, I lifted the cloth. "Oh, Marian, your homemade oatmeal bread and those dainty heart cakes. How do you manage to always come up with something special?" I asked. With the cakes still warm and frosting soft, the answer was clear. Marian had simply taken time to prepare a treat.

Warmed by Marian's heating pad, head propped on a freshly fluffed pillow, I soon forgot all discomfort, lost in the pages of a book of another time and place. I often wondered if Marian didn't have a sort of trouble barometer in her kitchen. She seemed to know our needs before we fully did ourselves. We should have been looking after her as her arthritis worsened. I knew that the unsteadiness of her wrists made it hard for her to manage kettles and twist-off bottle caps, but she found a way around these problems just as she solved ours.

Four years later, on Gail's wedding day, Marian's flower arrangements decorated each room of our home for the reception—her gift to the bride. As the last guest left and Marian tidied a table strewn with fern wisps, I took her swollen hand in mine. "Dear Marian, how can I ever thank you or repay you for all your many gifts over the years?" I asked. "The way we are transferred around the country, I may not be available to help you when you need it."

"Don't worry about that, Ceil," she answered, patting my hand. "We're all part of God's plan. It has been my joy to be able to help you in little ways, perhaps. You in turn will have a chance to help another; whether it is me or someone else doesn't really matter. God will send someone to me in my need. You see, it's a chain reaction, this passing back and forth of love."

She did move to Florida and is now wheelchair-bound, and

we were transferred to Saint Paul. I have tried to pass on her gifts and her story, meanwhile, praying that someone is helping her.

Just yesterday, a letter arrived from London from a girl we once took into our home for a week when her need was great. In the letter Margo says, "Remember once you told me how to repay you—by doing the same for someone else? I did it for that dear friend of mine who died from cancer last year. Many nights I dream about her and there is an emptiness without her. Yet, I shall always remember her, brown eyes so full of pain and yet also love, looking up at me full of tears, asking the same question. I gave her the answer you once gave me (Marian's love law). She thought a moment, then said, 'Oh, I know, I'll befriend the little old lady down the street who has everything, yet nothing without love.' There was Ginny in such a state, dying and yet wanting to give herself away. She taught me much through her unselfish ways. What I'm trying to say is that I've found your secret, and my prayer life has changed as I now pray, 'Let Christ be seen in me and let me lose myself in trying to show his love to others.' "

This is the great adventure. From our rendezvous points with God, he weaves our lives into a glowing fabric that shines for him. Catherine Marshall said, "The measure of a life is how much will you be missed?"[2]

A little old lady in Scotland was asked how she felt about death. She replied, "What does it matter? While I am here, God is with me; when I die, I shall be with Him."

Neither race, nor age, nor place, nor time can keep us from God if we seek his face. To be apart from God is death. To be in Christ is life.

NOTES

CHAPTER 1

1. Maurice Maeterlinck, *The Blue Bird* (New York: Dodd, Mead and Co., 1909).

CHAPTER 3

1. Catherine Marshall, *Beyond Our Selves* (New York: McGraw-Hill, 1961).

CHAPTER 4

1. Madame Chiang Kai-shek, *The Sure Victory* (Old Tappan, N.J.: Fleming H. Revell, 1955).
2. Madame Chiang Kai-shek, *Sure Victory,* pp. 32-33.

CHAPTER 5

1. Ceil McLeod, "Me Third," *Today,* February 4, 1968.

CHAPTER 6

1. Catherine Marshall, *Beyond Our Selves* (New York: McGraw-Hill, 1961), pp. 39-44, 82-83, and 201-216.
2. From the author's article, "God Uses Our Blunders Too," *Today,* January 28, 1968. Used by permission.

CHAPTER 7

1. *Good News for Modern Man–The New Testament in Today's English Version* (New York: American Bible Society, 1966).
2. From the author's article, "Can God Lift the Empire State Building?" *Today,* March 30, 1969. Used by permission.

CHAPTER 8

1. From the author's article, "Room in the Inn," *Today,* October 25, 1970. Used by permission.

CHAPTER 10

1. Jawaharlal Nehru, *The Discovery of India,* ed, R. I. Crane (New York: Anchor, Doubleday, 1960).
2. E. Stanley Jones, *The Christ of the Indian Road* (New York: Abingdon, 1925).

CHAPTER 12

1. Paul Tournier, "A Place for You," *Guideposts,* June 1966.
2. Catherine Marshall, *Beyond Our Selves* (New York: McGraw-Hill, 1961), Introduction.

DATE DUE